MW01241865

From Diapers to Death Row

J. Edward Sellers

To: Brian

J. Edward Sellers

From Diapers to Death Row

Copyright © 2020 by J. Edward Sellers
ISBN: 978-1-63073-338-4

Would you like to contact the author?
You can email him at
sweetchili401@gmail.com

All rights reserved.

No part of this publication may be reproduced or transmitted in any form or by any means electronic or mechanical, including photocopy, recording, or any information storage and retrieval system now known or to be invented, without permission in writing from the publisher, except by a reviewer who wishes to quote brief passages in connection with a review written for inclusion in a magazine, newspaper, website, or broadcast.

All Scripture quotations are taken from the Holy Bible, Authorized Version—King James Bible—preserved pure from the original autographs by divine providence. Copyright © Eternity by God Almighty. Used by permission.

Published in the United States of America

24 23 22 21 20   1 2 3 4 5

Table of Contents

Dedication

I am dedicating this book to my wife, Patricia Grace Sellers.

She has shown great patience with me among all the crazy years of working with high-risk kids and families, especially when I was on-call 24 hours a day!

Patricia continues to show amazing courage and a positive attitude in all the physical challenges she has been through and continues to go through year in and year out. Her graciousness and hospitality to others in the midst of her pain is a real model to all who know her and experience her presence!

She has been so wonderful to give extra time to our little dog, Demus, daddy's boy, so that I can spend the time necessary to complete this book. And what a tremendous unconditional love little Demus gives to both of us every day!

I also want to dedicate this book to the hundreds of youth I have had the privilege to work with for over 30 years. I am most honored that they have allowed me into their lives. I have learned so much from them despite the many bad choices we both have made at times. They have shown me that the human spirit the good Lord has given enables us, by His grace, to be overcomers and people who can learn from our mistakes and sinful choices and become the people that God intended us to be. To God be the glory, great things He has done!

Nothing gives me more joy than to hear of another former student who has "turned the corner" and is leading a productive, responsible life!

Acknowledgments

No project like this book can ever happen without the assistance of others with a variety of gifts and skills that enable you to produce a quality product.

I want to thank Linda Huff, an award-winning artist from Hawaii, for producing the front and back cover of this book.

Also, I am most indebted to Jim Mays, who agreed to be the primary editor. He has been a tremendous help.

I would like to thank the following people who agreed to read and respond to the first draft: Carolyn Sellers, June Carlson and her husband, Mike Brogan.

Much thanks to Jennifer Hastings, who typed the final copy, and special thanks for the help and assistance of my publisher, Jim Wendorf of Faithful Life Publishers.

Foreword

This book covers over 30 years of working with high-risk kids and families and my relationship with two faith-based organizations and one denomination. I seek to integrate my faith journey with the many experiences that I have had along the way with what may be called a sub-culture of American life.

I know now, more than ever, that whatever I have accomplished in this life, it has been all God's doing! If left to myself, I would be a total failure. I would not have the power to be an overcomer, but for His grace and mercy. I never want anyone to think that John Sellers is anything but a "sinner saved by grace!"

I believe that most Christians, like Peter, David, and Moses in the Bible, have had a time in their lives when, like Humpty Dumpty, they have had a great fall. Their new nature becomes overwhelmed by their fallen nature. It is not a good thing, but it can lead to a good outcome when repentance is followed by God's ability to rebuild your life, enabling you to learn a hard lesson and apply the principle of abiding in the Spirit of God daily. God enables us to see the visions and dream the dreams that He has for us to accomplish by His power—to see Him make the mission impossible, possible! That's the exciting life that the Lord has for all of us. Some experience this more than others, but every person who really takes God at His word and moves out in faith can see Him work mission impossible in their lives, and that is what makes life bearable and exciting!

I have seen in my life, and in the lives of others, that what Satan intends for evil, God turns around for good and gets us to the place He wants us to be; this makes all the difference in the world.

It is my deep desire to inspire as many people as I can to get involved with high-risk kids and families in their communities as volunteer mentors or institutional volunteers. Some of you may feel led to make this a vocational choice. If so, I will be doubly blessed!

The average boy in a juvenile unit throughout this country has had five or more father figures in his life by the time he is 15 years of age. Many of these men are live-in boyfriends of the boy's mom. Only about one-third of institutionalized teen boys have a relationship with their biological father, and even when they do, it is often not a good relationship. Also, a high percentage of troubled teens, both male and female, have been sexually abused multiple times by the time they are 17 years of age. Very few of these young people have what could be called a normal childhood. Often, they are forced to be the adult in the family by the time they are 12 years of age.

To enable one of these troubled young men to catch his first fish, go on his first canoe trip, climb his first mountain, or make his first foil-wrapped "hobo stew"— that, for me, has been one of the most fulfilling times of my life! I haven't been able to raise any kids of my own, but the Lord has enabled me to have a part in raising and influencing thousands of young men, as well as a few troubled young women, over these many years. To God be the glory, great things He has done!

If just a handful of people decide to get involved directly with high-risk kids and families after reading this book, I will consider the hours spent in writing well worth it!

I Remember Ma Ma Kay

Years ago, there was a weekly tv series called, *I Remember Ma Ma*. It didn't last too long as I recall, but it centered around an inspiring mother and the many good memories that one of her children had about her life. Many of the young men I have worked with can tell you very little about their biological fathers, but most of them have good things to say about their moms and grandmothers who raised them. The sad part of this is that it is very difficult for single-parent moms to raise sons without

a dad in the home. Often, they are bringing in one boyfriend after another, and this doesn't usually do anything but increase the problems. It takes a strong and amazing woman to raise her children to grow up to be mature and responsible, so although my mom didn't have to raise my siblings and I alone, she was an amazing woman in so many ways and served as a good model for her children and for many other moms, both in the church and in the community.

My mother, Kathryn Ritzman Sellers Reeder, was born in Reading, Pennsylvania. She had one older brother and one younger brother. Her mother passed away at a young age when my mom was about ten years old. Her dad, Orson Ritzman, married a second time soon after his first wife, Carrie, died.

Mother described herself as a bit of a tomboy at this time in her life. She would often come home from school with a bloody nose from fighting. Her second mom did not care much for children, especially not for tomboys like Kathryn, who was called Kittie by her family, so Mom was sent to live with her Aunt Bessie in Collingswood, New Jersey until she was 18 years old.

Being sent away from her father and brothers deeply disturbed my mother and her older brother, Nevin, yet it was while living with her Aunt Bessie that my mom was taken to the Collingswood Methodist Church where she was introduced to the gospel message and she prayed to give her life to Jesus. My mom had a wonderful Sunday School teacher who took a personal interest in her and mentored her in the Word of God and in some basic principles of Christian living. Her Aunt Bessie was a good role model as well and treated my mom as one of her own children.

In the summertime, Mom would visit her dad and her two uncles in Pottsville and Pottstown, Pennsylvania. Her Uncle Bob was the milkman and iceman in Pottsville, so Mom got to ride on the milk wagon pulled by horses to deliver ice and milk to a large number of homes throughout the town. Uncle Bob had no children of his own, so he and his wife loved having Mom with them for about a month every summer. Her other uncle had a saloon, so when she visited him, she would get a glass of birch beer!

One of the things my mother learned early in her faith journey was that God is always trustworthy. She believed and practiced all her life that God can be trusted to work all things out. It was her way of applying God's sovereignty to her life and to all her family challenges. The longer I have lived, the more I see how I have adopted this principle in my life as well. I have been able to face my failures, the rejections, and the hard times in my life, including the death of my younger brother, Bob, at the age of 59, with a deep realization that God is in control!

It is important to note that even though her dad was quick to farm her out to her aunt, my mom was quick to take him in after his third wife passed away in 1973. (Her dad outlived three wives!) I think she wanted her dad to know that she had forgiven him for farming her out to her aunt, and she wanted to demonstrate the love of Christ when the other members of her family held this against him all their lives. She took care of him for about a year before he passed away in his mid-eighties.

My dad had passed away after a long illness not long before Mom took in her dad. It was not a convenient time, but as usual, Mom didn't do things when it was convenient. Her desire was always to do what she could to meet the needs of others and to invest in them.

When my grandfather lived with us, Mom took him to Calvary Church in Charlotte, North Carolina, most Sundays. He loved going to Melvin Graham's (Billy Graham's brother) men's Sunday School, where he heard good Bible teaching along with the gospel message. Just before he passed away, he told Mom that Jesus was his pilot. The family understood that to mean he was following Jesus; this was very encouraging to Mom.

When my mother was still young, she attended Collingswood High School, the same school that Michael Landon (*The Little House on the Prairie*) attended! She majored in secretarial courses and shorthand. After this, at the age of 18, she moved south with her friend, Joyce, and Joyce's mother to Charlotte. My mother, Joyce, and Joyce's mother moved into a large boarding house and got one large room upstairs with no central heat. Along with using several blankets to keep warm, Mom told me that she would wrap up a hot iron in a towel and put it at the foot of the large bed where they all slept.

My mother lived during the difficult times in the US and around the world when folks were trying to recover from the Depression and were seeking to stay out of a war with Hitler, who was growing more and more powerful as the leader of Germany. It was during this time that my mother signed up as a volunteer at the Charlotte Rescue Mission. The mission sought to assist men who were out of work, along with those who were struggling with alcohol issues.

One night, my dad, John Alton Sellers, who grew up on a small farm close to Rocky Mount, North Carolina, ventured into the Rescue Mission, looking for a meal and a place to sleep for the night. He had come to Charlotte looking for work, but he found the gospel and my mom as well. My dad had responded to the gospel message at the Rescue Mission and became a believer, and throughout their courtship, my parents attended a young couples Bible study group. Years later, my dad was asked to be on the board of directors of the Charlotte Rescue Mission, and after his death, the boardroom was named in his memory!

My parents were married in the home of Pastor Ed Hancox, who served as an assistant pastor at Calvary Presbyterian Church, Independent. My middle name, Edward, came from their strong friendship with Pastor Ed. Soon after their marriage, my parents moved to a small cottage home in Asheville, North Carolina.

My dad worked for a faith-based company, C. B. Drug Company in Harrisburg, North Carolina. He traveled throughout North and South Carolina selling items such as saccharin sweetener and other drug store items. My dad was forced to quit school in the 8th grade to help run the farm after his mom died. This was a real setback for him, from which he never recovered. He worked hard and taught his children about the value of hard work and work ethic, but with his limited education, he was never able to get a well-paying job.

One day, my mom was hanging out clothes to dry in the backyard. She had Joe, her first child, my older brother, with her. On her way into the back door of the house, she saw a large rattlesnake on the back steps. She ran next door to get her neighbor to kill the snake. My mother was deathly afraid of snakes, so when my dad came home from work that evening, my mom told him loud and clear, "We are moving tomorrow!" There was no discussion. They moved the very next day!

When my brother, Joe, was a teenager, he played a joke on our mother one Saturday when she was preparing to mop the kitchen floor. He took a realistic-looking rubber snake and curled it up under the kitchen table. Soon, we heard a blood-curdling scream coming from the kitchen. Joe heard her and came into the kitchen laughing his head off. Mom let him know, in no uncertain terms, that it would be the last joke played on her! Joe was ordered to take the snake out of the house and throw it in the garbage. Joe came very close to sleeping out in the backyard that night! He soon apologized and told her he would never do anything like that again.

When Joe was still a young boy, my dad was called into the Army and was sent to Germany. Mom took Joe with her to live with her dad in Reading, Pennsylvania. She worked with her dad at this AAA Travel Agency until my dad returned from the war. Since Joe was the only one of my siblings born before the war, he was much older than the rest of us. He is seven years older than my sister Kristina, eight years older than me, and twelve years older than my younger brother Bob, who was the baby of the family, yet the first of the siblings to pass away at the age of 59.

My mother loved to work. Not long after my dad returned from the war, my mom became the executive secretary at J. N. Pease Associates, an architectural and engineering company in Charlotte. This firm had the contract for Duke University and designed many of the buildings on that campus for many years.

Mom's first job when she moved to Charlotte was with the Department of the Navy. When she interviewed for the job, she was asked how fast she could take dictation. She thought a few seconds and said, "Well, when you go fast, I go fast, and when you go slow, I go slow." The interviewer laughed and said, "You've got the job!"

My mom and dad were charter members of Calvary Presbyterian Church, Independent. They took their faith and their membership at Calvary seriously. My dad was a deacon and an elder in the church when he passed away from kidney failure in 1972. As a deacon, he was very consistent in taking care of the widows of the church and would meet with them soon after they lost their husbands to see that they got the assistance they needed. He made sure that their transition from being married to being single again went as well as possible.

Many widows in that day had been very dependent on their husbands. Many of them didn't drive a car, and some didn't handle any of the family finances, either. They didn't cut grass or do any heavy yard work. For a woman in this situation, it was frightening when her husband passed. My dad realized this and spent many Saturdays helping the latest widow in the church with yard work and getting the assistance she needed with her finances. Since my dad travelled each week in his work, weekends were very important to him and his family. So, at times, this need he felt to help the widows put pressure on his relationships and the time needed with his family.

My dad was also a member of Gideons International. This organization distributed Bibles in motels, hotels, schools, doctor's offices, and jails all over the country. My dad accepted the responsibility of bringing New Testaments and sharing his story at the Charlotte Mecklenburg jail two Sundays a month. He occasionally took me with him when I became old enough.

All of us kids were taught the meaning of dedication by just watching my parent's dedication to their jobs and their church. Many Saturday nights, I would see my mom out at her desk in the living room, preparing her Sunday School lesson for her fourth-grade boys' class. She taught this class for about 25 years!

My mom loved seeing and meeting specific needs that weren't being met in her church. She noticed that there weren't any youth group meetings on Sunday evenings for the fourth, fifth, and sixth grades (the junior class). The church had groups for junior high and senior high but not for the juniors, so Mom got permission to start "Joys and Jets." Mom would challenge those who attended Joys and Jets to bring an object each week, and she would give a sermonette on that object the following week. This was a hilarious exercise to us older kids in the family, but we had to be careful not to joke too much in front of Mom, as she took this very seriously! Mom went on to play a major role in starting three other ministries in the church, even in her seventies!

After becoming single again when my dad passed away at the age of 59, Mom felt led to join with others in forming a city-wide Sunday night singles group that met at Calvary Church. This group grew quite large and drew singles from all over Charlotte. These folks would bring their children to the youth groups at Calvary while they attended the adult singles group. Mother served as the secretary of this singles group and she worked hard at getting to know as many of those who attended as possible. Whenever she heard one of those attending mention a need they had, Mom would work to get them connected to some person or some ministry that could help meet that need. She desired that everyone feel welcome, so she introduced them to others who were regular attenders.

I could go on and on about the many church activities that my mom worked with or helped set up, including the last one she started in her seventies called, "Morning Glories," a monthly support group for widows, but the thing that impressed me from a family standpoint was the way that Ma Ma Kay worked so hard to treat all her children equally. She wanted all her children and grandchildren to be successful. When we brought our report cards home to show her, she would only ask us one question, "Did you do your very best?" To her, if a C or a C+ was the best you felt you could do, that was fine with her, but she knew when we knew when a grade was not the best we could do. That, in itself, made us work harder!

For the 22 years when "Kay" (her office name) worked at J. N. Pease Associates, we kids would always pray each year that the company would have a good year because in December, all the employees would get a yearly bonus check. When the company had a good year, Mom's bonus check would be between $500 and $600. When the year was not so good, her check would be about $250.

The yearly bonus was what Mom used for making Christmas happen for her four children. She would carefully split most of the bonus money into four equal amounts, about $75 to $100 per child. This amount would determine what we would get from Santa on our wish list!

Mom would only get one bicycle per year. She began with the oldest kid and worked down to the youngest. That meant I was the third in line for a bike. I will never forget the year that it was my turn for a bike. I got a beautiful red and white bike. It was my personal "Impala," since I loved Chevy Impala cars the best. I "drove" that Impala all over the neighborhood and saw my territory extend quite a bit because of my new wheels.

It was only when it was your turn to get a bike that you knew what you were getting that Christmas, unless you were my sister Kris! She had to know before Christmas Day what she was getting. So, while my mom was at work, my sister would check my mom's bedroom closet and would even go up into the attic to find what she was getting. But she couldn't keep it to herself and had to tell the rest of her siblings at least one day before Christmas. The word would get back to Mom, and she would get so upset because, to her, the best part of Christmas was being surprised on Christmas Day! Several times, my mom would come close to taking Kris's presents back to the store and putting coal in my sister's stocking!

Mom taught me to be sensitive to the needs of others and to be available to say a word in season, as it were, when the Lord opened a door to do so. I remember her telling me in confidence about a neighbor lady who shared with her that her husband had begun drinking more and more on the weekends. When he drank, he became angry and threatened her and her young son. It seems this neighbor felt safe talking with my mom about her problem, and as far as I can tell, she didn't share this with anyone else in the community or church.

One day, she told my mom that it was so bad that she had to resort to locking her son up in his room and going out and locking herself in the storage closet off the back porch of the house. She would stay there most of the night and come out when she was pretty sure her husband would be asleep. My mom prayed with her that the Lord would give her wisdom to know what to do.

My neighbor talked with a lawyer and decided she had to take her son and leave. She knew that her husband adored his son and loved to teach him things when he wasn't drinking. One day, just after her husband left for work, a moving van arrived. She took the furniture she needed for herself and her son and moved close to her family about 100 miles away. She left a note telling her husband that once she could be convinced that he had received the help he needed to get and stay off alcohol, she would come back and live with him again. I was glad to see not too long after this, she and her son came back, and she never had to leave again.

My mom was very dedicated to us four kids and wanted us to have some vacation experiences during the summer like the other kids in the neighborhood. We had very little extra money, so my mom depended on the Lord to provide in a special way to make summer vacations happen.

A lady where mom worked had, along with her husband, built several nice cottages on Ocean Island Beach off the North Carolina coast. You had to take a ferry boat to get out to this little island. It was sparsely populated when we were kids, but now that a bridge connects the island to the mainland, it is crowded with cabins and businesses.

This lady heard that my mom was looking for a place to take her kids for vacation, and she offered one of her cabins to my mom for about $75 to $100 per week as long as we cleaned it up nicely before we left. We loved going to this island for several summers and enjoying what was pretty much a private beach, with very few people around.

Another lady in our church also realized that our family did not have the extra money needed to take all six of us on a vacation, so she offered Mom the use of her nice mountain house in Blowing Rock, North Carolina. This place was just one block off the main street in beautiful Blowing Rock. It had three bedrooms, two baths, and a big covered front porch. She only asked Mom for $100 per week! Again, we saw the Lord meet our needs just as my mom always told us He would. In so many ways, it seemed to be over and abundant what we could ever have expected.

My mom didn't drive, but she began to realize that my dad's health was getting progressively worse. So, at 42, she made up her mind that she was going to learn to drive. My dad didn't have much time to teach her as he was gone most of the week for his job and was very busy on the weekends. He also was not gifted with a lot of patience, so my mom would get up early and go out with my older brother on his paper route. She would drive him around to practice her driving. It was a good time as few people were on the road and my brother, Joe, adored his mom and had a lot more patience with her than my dad.

My dad got his first new car in 1957. It was a '57 Chevy with a straight drive on the steering wheel. As an 8-year-old, this was the most exciting day of my life. I got up as early as I could that Saturday morning after my dad had brought the car home late Friday night. I ran to the kitchen window and looked out on the driveway to see that shiny new blue and white Chevy!

I quickly ate my breakfast and dashed out to sit in the car, smell the new car smell, and pretend to drive it. I came in for lunch but went back out to "drive" it some more until my dad could be talked into giving me a ride. However, the problem was that it was straight drive, so when you had to stop at a stoplight on a hill, as we did when we went to church each Sunday, it was impossible for my mom to learn how to use the clutch properly to engage the gear without rolling back. My dad would have to get out and drive us the rest of the way to church, to my mom's disgust.

It wasn't long before my mom convinced my dad to get a 1958 Ford with automatic drive. With that, she was off and going, and she soon had her driver's license. But since she had begun to learn to drive with a clutch, she now drove with one foot on the gas and the other resting above the brake. No matter how hard we tried to teach her to only use one foot, she used two feet for the rest of her driving career!

My mom was about 81 when she was still working part-time at Calvary Church in Charlotte. She was driving quite a distance back and forth to work—sometimes by herself and sometimes with another lady. One day on the way home, Mom had a fainting spell. The other friend with her was able to grab the wheel and keep them from having an accident, but it became clear to the family that Mom was going to have to give up the car. The problem was that Mom's attitude was she just had to get on the right pill or other solution so she could continue driving.

My brother, Bob, was good at coming up with answers, and she trusted him more than the rest of us, so when Bob told her that her granddaughter, Carrie, had just graduated from college and needed a car to get to her teaching job, Mom was quick to "loan" Carrie her car. Bob promised he or her other son, Joe, would get her anywhere she wanted to go. She also had another neighbor friend just a few houses down who was willing to take her to the store when she needed groceries or something else. The problem was solved, and soon after, Mom moved into a retirement apartment that served meals and even had a hairdresser to do her hair.

By this time, Mom began to be a bit forgetful: she started a few small kitchen fires in her apartment, so it was made clear to the family that she would have to go into assisted living. She accepted this, and we found a nice place in beautiful South Charlotte. She had a lively roommate who she enjoyed living with, and it was not long before she was telling us about how they got popcorn and watched the Charlotte Panthers play football. She would tell me how they did each week and why they won or lost the game.

After four or five years, Mom was getting more and more dependent, and her mind was getting worse. Again, Bob had the skill to know how to talk to Mom about going into memory care. He told her that he was having a kidney transplant, and it would be a long-term commitment, so he would not be available to assist her for several months. He was told there was one room available at the memory care unit that was across the parking lot from Mom's assisted living. Mom agreed to go into the memory care unit, where she could get more care while he was going through his long-term kidney surgery and recovery.

In the end, Bob did not live through this, as he got infections and passed away at the age of 59. It was one of the most difficult days of my life, when my sister, Kris, and I went to see Mom to tell her that Bobby had been given less than a week to live. Her youngest child was going to pass away before she did.

We took Mom out to the garden behind her living place to tell her the news. Her mind was about as sharp as it had been in a long time that day. She asked the obvious question, "Why him and not me? I should go first, not Bobby." After a few tears, we began to pray. Kris prayed, and then I prayed. We didn't expect Mom to pray. We had not heard her pray for several years at this time in her life. But on that day, the Lord gave her good understanding, and she prayed a very simple prayer. She thanked the Lord for giving her such a wonderful son, who had invested so much time with her for so many years. She gave him back to the Lord, and it was such a special, precious time.

A week later, Bobby went to be with his Lord. Mom attended his memorial at Calvary Church, which included a meal, a reception time, and a service. This lasted four hours. I was amazed at how well my mom held up the whole time.

The last time I was able to talk to my mom was when I visited her at the memory care unit where she was living. When I arrived, Mom was sitting with another lady at the front door. She never sat out there, so when I entered, I asked her why she was sitting out there. She told me that she was waiting for the taxi to take her home, so I asked her if I could sit and talk with her until the taxi got there. She said yes, so I sat beside her and had a very positive talk with her for about 30 minutes. When I could tell that she was tired of talking, I said goodbye and told her that I hoped the taxi would come soon. After leaving, I realized that Mom was not waiting for a taxi, she was waiting for a chariot!

It was not long before the "taxi" came for Mom. We were notified that she was sleeping and had not woken for several days. She was on hospice care and was being kept peaceful and out of pain. My wife Pat and I slept just outside her door in comfortable chairs all night. The next morning, my sister and sister-in-law arrived, and we sat with Mom as she took her last breath. I held her hand, sang to her, and told her it was alright for her to go home. She did. Mom passed into glory at the age of 96! After a lifetime of taking care of others and seeking to meet so many unmet needs, Mom was able to look into the face of her Savior and have all her needs met completely for eternity!

Mom was an amazing woman, and she will continue to have an impact on my life every time I remember how hard she worked and how much she loved to work always trusting the Lord to provide and to make things work out. "He is going to work things out," my mom would always say, and I can say, in much agreement with my mom, "Yes, Mom, He has and is working things out to bring about His purposes in our lives, just as He did in yours."

Ma Ma Kay's Short Story on Her Life

My mother died when I was at the very tender and delicate age of nine years old. Before that time, my childhood was filled with beautiful memories: memories of camping trips, trips to the beach, picnics in the parks, long walks, and walks in the rain (my favorite). Each day was a wonderful surprise—going on all-day business trips with my dad, getting up early in the morning and going to the market, playing baseball on hot summer days (I was a bit of a tomboy for a while), hide and seek on warm summer nights, my favorite boyfriend riding me around on his bike, Sunday dinners with all the aunts, uncles, and cousins present, and each on taking his turn to say "God bless this food, Amen!" Yes, we were a wonderful family.

Then, BOOM! Mother was ill just a short time—three weeks to be exact—then she was gone. Things changed drastically. Shortly thereafter, my dad married again and for me, he too was gone. Gone were all the good times we had, and everything changed dramatically.

Now, what did I have to stand on? To lose someone you love so much at such a tender age and have your life totally turned about overnight was torture. It was almost too much for a little girl, but God had me in His hand—He saw my future. During this time, I was a very unhappy little girl. I began to lose weight. My father was busy with his new wife—in fact, so busy he just didn't have time anymore for me.

However, he was determined the children would not be separated. I had an older brother and a baby brother who was just a year old when our mother died, so relatives could not take us at the time.

Then, there came a time when we visited my stepmother's family. Her sister, who became my second mother, loved children and was especially fond of girls. She had three of her own. She had health problems, and after several visits, her husband asked me how I would like to live with them and help with the younger girls. I was eleven at the time. I had liked it there when I had visited previously. The atmosphere was so much different than at home, and I readily consented that I wanted to stay and go to school there. So, by the fall of 1929, I was all settled in my new home and shared a bedroom with the oldest girl.

My own relatives had not been asked if they would like for me to live with them, so they were terribly hurt. Also, my two brothers stayed at home. I didn't realize this at first, but later, I found out the separation was very hard for me to be away from them, especially my older brother, with whom I had been very close. My baby brother also meant a lot to me.

I started going to Sunday School and church almost immediately. It was a very sound church, and my Sunday School teacher was the church secretary. At first, I thought she was very strict and strait-laced, and she was, but I found her to be very sincere. It wasn't long until Decision Day at church, and I went forward to accept Christ. I know that at the time I really didn't know what it was all about; all I knew was I wanted Jesus in my heart. I didn't want to go to Hell; I wanted to go to Heaven, so I went forward. That was the first step and the most necessary step that we must all take—opening our hearts to Him and moving out.

Having the same Spirit-filled teacher for several years meant a lot to me in my spiritual growth. Then, as I entered high school, I moved into another department, and there, the Lord again gave me another wonderful teacher. She was a totally different person as far as personality goes, but she was also a Spirit-filled and totally dedicated Christian. She was dark haired, dark skinned, and had a little Indian blood. She had a beautiful smile, was full of fun, and was very tall. She had been a Girl Scout leader for several years. We would meet at her home one afternoon a week after school. There, we would bring our problems and talk them over and get down on our knees and pray about them. When we were done with the serious things, we had a fun time and refreshments.

During this time, my spiritual grow grew by leaps. I really wanted to be what the Lord wanted me to be. I stood firm and steadfast for Him. I had many trials in school and many temptations. I had to stand alone a lot and do without a lot of friends, but I knew if they didn't love the Lord, and did not want to go His way, they were not the companions I should have, though they were always my friends at school. I was close to them, even though they thought I was foolish to take the stand that I did. It wasn't easy to say no to dancing parties and not be a part of the "in" crowd, yet the Lord fulfilled my life. I would say that this beautiful teacher meant more than anything in my life. I can see her sweet, happy, and serious face before me whenever I feel the least bit low and need to be lifted up. She was just a radiant Christian.

It was still very hard for me to be away from my father and two brothers and to not have a real mother. I spent many lonely hours. I always went to my room and read my Bible and prayed that God would help me through these periods and make me strong. I also knew that my father lived in a different world than mine. He had good jobs, a lot of friends, and was well known. He took nice trips, but he did not know the Lord. I would often think, "Oh, if mother could have only lived, and I could have been brought up in this atmosphere." But I did not dwell on this aspect of my life very long, for I knew all that was in vain. If one did not know the Savior, then I would rather things be like they were. I once had a very lovely bedroom with all my own beautiful furniture in it, and now, I was sharing a very small bedroom with not much furniture at all, but I was sharing a home with a lot of love in it—that was worth it!

I must say that I had a lot of disappointments in my Christian life as a teenager, but I am sure that this was part of my growth. If I had all my prayers answered like I wanted them, I am sure I would not have become the strong Christian I needed to be to cope with circumstances in later years.

I prayed much for my brothers, especially my younger, as he was just a year old when Mother died. When I went home in the summer to visit, I always tried to be a "little mother" to him. I mended and washed his clothes and, in general, just took him under my wing. Then, when he joined the service at 17, I really prayed earnestly for him, and the Lord answered my prayers and took care of him the whole eight years he was in the Armed Forces.

Due to my background of sadness, I was not the outgoing teenager that I might have been otherwise. As a little girl, before the death of my mother, I was "Miss Personality Plus." I had even given elocution lessons. I was a very good performer—memorizing long verses of poetry, and I did quite a lot of recitation work. But, as my life changed so drastically during those crucial years, I developed a bit of an inferiority complex. You see, my uncle was made my guardian. He needed to be this as there were certain papers connected with school that he, at times, had to sign for me. But I always hated to have a guardian. I wanted my own dad. I would think, "I have a daddy, yet I don't have one." My uncle always had to be the stand-in, and although I appreciated this and loved him, I still wanted my own father to be there. It just did something to me that I can't explain. Losing a mother and a father at almost the same time was just too much to take, except the Lord made me determined.

I think a teenage girl always goes through that period in life, wondering whether a boy will ask her for a date or hoping for romance. I knew with the stand I had taken, it sure would be hard. I wouldn't be asked at school unless I met a real Christian young man. I would have to meet him through church activities. There was one I had my eye on at church, and, low and behold, he asked me if I would go out on a blind double date with two other couples. Of course, he had his date, and I was to have the blind date and go with him. This wasn't what I wanted, but I thought I would take the chance since the others were Christians. But I didn't know about the blind date.

Four of us were in the back seat of the car. The one I was really interested in was also in the back seat. I wanted to act great to show him that I was the kind of Christian girl he would really like to date. However, as fate would have it, the date I got was the mushy type. He wanted to kiss me every time he thought he had the chance. I brushed him off or literally held him off until one time, I thought maybe if I just give in to him one time, he will leave me alone. That was the wrong thing to do, I later found out. He decided o give me a kiss to make up for all the others he didn't get. To make a long story short, I was mad and embarrassed, too, because I wanted to make such a good impression on the other one, the very special one. Now, he would think I let every Tom, Dick, and Harry kiss me. And sure enough, he had nothing to do with me after that. Well, that was a lesson I had to learn—be determined to not give in.

As I mentioned at the beginning of my story, I went to live in a home with three younger girls. Of course, as each year went by, these girls began to grow and mature, and I wanted to do my part to show them what a real Christian is like in my actions and deeds. This I did in many ways. We all four took turns doing the dishes every night. Although I was a little older, I didn't really care to do dishes any more than anyone else. However, I often took someone else's turn so she could do something else. Or, I would wash the pots and pans (none of us liked to do the pots and pans), even though it was not my turn to do them. I also helped them with their clothes—ironed, mended, and helped them with lessons. And when one was very ill and had to stay out of school for a whole year, I tutored her a lot, so she was able to go back to school the next year without missing out. I often walked back from the grocery store after walking a couple of miles home from school, not only once, but often, twice. The others didn't want to do it, and rather than have a fuss, I would do it, knowing the Lord would give me the strength to do it. I would set the example! The others were a good bit younger.

When I was a junior in high school, I wanted to teach a Sunday School class of girls more than anything else. I wanted to copy my dark-haired, smiling teacher. I would be the best teacher anywhere around. I asked the Christian Education Department about teaching, but they had a rule that you could not teach until you had graduated from high school. I patiently waited and got my class; I was determined. However, just when I got my class, I found out that I had to leave the home I had lived in for the past seven years. I was disappointed about giving up the class when I had waited a long time to get it, but I knew I had to trust the Lord in all things.

We were going through the Depression, and jobs were very scarce. I was at the top of my commercial class and a champion typist. However, there weren't any jobs available. After moving from relative to relative, I lived with my dad for a short time. I had an invitation to visit some friends in the south (Charlotte). I was determined, if it was the Lord's will, that I would get a job in the south, and there I would remain, unless the Lord showed me differently.

My father dropped me off on his way to Florida for a vacation. If I did not have a job when he returned, he would pick me up and take me home. I was determined to not let this happen. I prayed and earnestly went about seeking employment. First, I checked in at the employment office, then the newspaper company, among others. As a last resort, I chose a street and went in one office after another. I, at least, would do my part, and I knew God would do His.

Faith without works is dead. Three weeks were up, and my dad came by. I did not have a job yet, but I had some good promises, so he left me a little more money and told me to try for a week or two more, and then, if I didn't have anything, he would send me money to come back up north. Even through all this, I felt confident the Lord was going to give me something, and He did!

In a short while, the employment office called me and said they had a job for me. Finally, the day and hour for me to go for my interview came along with a terrible storm, but I knew I had to get that job if this was the one for me. I was there on time, soaking wet, but there! This was in my favor. There was nothing in the building but a few desk and chairs. I was thrown a wet pad of telegram blanks and told to sit down and take a letter. I have to admit I did a little praying right then. Taking shorthand on a wet telegram blank made me a little nervous, to say the least.

But I was determined and apparently did alright, for he told me I was hired. How thankful I was that I got that job! Little did I know at the time that the position I had accepted with a "Trailer Co." was not about trailers that go on trucks or those pulled behind cars, but previews to movies. I did not actually go to work until a week after I was hired since they were in the process of moving in, so I did not know what the company was until later.

About a year prior to this time, I had made up my mind I would only go to good movies. I had turned it all over to the Lord, and I would not go to any movies because I did not want to be a bad example to anyone. If someone I was trying to be an example to saw me going into the movie house, that person would not know whether I was going to a good one or a bad one. I did not want to be a detriment to any weaker brothers or sisters. So here I was working for a movie company! I really was a little confused. Should I give it up right away? But I was sure that the Lord gave this job to me, and I really needed the money very badly. I told myself that previews weren't actual movies, but it was almost the same. But Lord, when you knew I just had made the decision to only go to a few good movies, why this? I decided the Lord must have a reason for my being there. So, I determined, with the Lord's help, to stay as long as He wanted me to stay. I would be a testimony there in the office where He placed me. Then, after being employed for a few months, I still had not settled the problem in my heart of whether I should give up going. Each person has to decide different things. What might bother some people, might not bother others. But I very much wanted to be what the Lord wanted me to be, and the movie question—to go or not—really bothered me.

Finally, one evening, I was alone in my bedroom, and I got down on my knees and told the Lord that no matter what, even if I lost my job, I was not going to attend any movies from then on, as I did not want to hurt my testimony. I was determined to follow Him. The sweetest peace came over my being that I have ever experienced either before or since. I felt I had truly been obedient to what He wanted for me at that time.

You must remember that I was still a teenager. I was away from home. I had no extra money, only what I made each week. Soon, at my job, they would have to find out that I didn't approve of movies. To me, most of them were not good. For me, to be a good example all the way around, I would have to forego the good ones and just not go to any.

(There was no tv at this time.) Well, it soon got out in the office, but the Lord took over. I had numerous occasions to give my testimony and to stand up for the Lord. I was an extremely good coworker, an excellent typist, personable, and eager to help anyone who had too much to do if I was caught up with my work. Instead of being fired, I was promoted twice. Raises were few and far between, but I received at least two that I can remember in the three years that I worded there. This was a small office of about 12 people, and they loved more than anything to tell dirty jokes. I would not listen, as I always abhorred them ever since I became a Christian. They were determined that I would hear them, and I was determined that I would not. You know who won? Me!

One little thing I must insert here. Back then, $18 a week was an extremely good wage for a secretary. The bookkeeper at the office with lots of experience only made $20. So, when I heard that everybody always got a Christmas bonus of $25, I was elated and knew I could do all my Christmas shopping with this and have some left over! Well, when it came time to give out the bonuses, I did not get one, but I got a raise. I had been making $16 a week, and now I would make $18 a week. But I didn't realize that if you got a raise, you didn't get the $25 Christmas bonus. This was too much for me. I had been counting on it so much. I just broke down there in the office and cried. I asked if I could have the bonus instead of the raise. They were very sorry, but it had come from the home office, and they had recommended me for the raise, and there was no way in the world that they could unrecommend me. Well, I don't remember how I bought my Christmas presents, but I'm sure everyone got a little remembrance, and I realized that the Lord wanted to teach me a lesson—to keep on trusting Him.

One time at the office, I met a very handsome man. He asked me on a date, and I accepted. Being very unwise in the ways of the world and not realizing that the ways of the world are very deceptive, I didn't know that someone in the office had set this date up for me. They knew just what this man was like and that he was not the type for me. But, not knowing this, and since he was very nice and very handsome, I fell into the trap. I dated him a couple times, and although I knew better, I let him kiss me goodnight. Then we had another date, but when he showed up, there was another couple in the car. I knew from the start that I didn't like this, but I went ahead and got in the car, and off we went. We had not gone very far before the gal in the front pulled out a bottle and took a drink. She offered it to me and the other fellow in the car. My date didn't take any though. I reminded him that I didn't drink and did not go for that sort of thing. He told them not to drink any more. Before I knew it, we were out of Charlotte and out into the country—goodness knows where. I asked him where we were going, and he said out to the river. Of course, this was at night, and I began praying, and praying I did. "Oh Lord, if you get me out of this situation, I am determined never to get back in it again." And I really meant it! I would be an old maid the rest of my life if I had to.

Finally, we drove up in front of a cabin. I did not want to get out of the car. The other couple got out and went over to the cabin. It was supposed to be unoccupied, but it was occupied, thank the Lord! It was occupied with about six men playing cards. Well, the men playing let them know that they had no intention of leaving. I also knew then what my escorts' intentions were! We walked around for a bit, but I begged him to take me home. I did not want to be out there, and I wanted to go home. So, in just a little while, we all got in the car and went home. That was the last date I had with that fellow, and I found out later that this was a put-up job trying to get me into trouble. Well, I was so thankful that everything worked out the way it did, but this could have been a different story! You see, even those who love the Lord, can get into trouble if they let down just a little. You must stay very close to the Lord and trust Him for all things.

Very shortly after this, I met a man who loved the Lord. It was a beautiful courtship. Money was scarce, but love was abundant. He didn't even have a car, but we never once gave it a thought about walking a couple of miles back and forth to church twice a day or walking wherever we wanted to go. In about a year and half, we were married. Money was still scarce, and our folks on both sides were far away, but that was good. We had to trust the Lord. I determined to be the best wife and mother anybody ever could want. Needless to say, I wanted to child just as soon as the Lord wanted to give me one. I knew He would provide, and He did. However, I wasn't expecting to be "expecting" so soon. I gave up my job to go to a mountain town to be closer to my husband, and I knew I could find work, but then I found out that I was pregnant with our first child.

During the months ahead, my faith was tried many times. I was ill for several long weeks, so I could not get another job, then later, when I was feeling better, it didn't seem in the best interest for me to work. My husband worked as a salesman on commission. His route was through the mountains, calling on stores in the small mountain towns. We had an especially hard winter with lots of ice and snow, and he could not get around much of the time, so money got even scarcer. But God led us to a little two-room apartment upstairs in a private home. It was so warm and cozy, and downstairs was the most excellent cook. She was a warm, friendly, elderly Christian woman who always made too much of everything she cooked and always baked an extra pie—more than was needed. My husband left early in the mornings and did not get home until late in the evenings. She always sent me dinner upstairs every day. Most of the time, there was plenty for my husband as well, and I saved it for him. She didn't know it (or she did) that sometimes we just didn't have any food.

Thanksgiving Day was almost near. Our first Thanksgiving, and our baby was due in three months, and money just gave out. We got our rent paid and other necessary bills, but there was nothing left for food, and here it was Thanksgiving. But I was determined to trust the Lord. I had lots of time to spend in God's Word, and this I did and prayed. I was at peace with the Lord, and I knew He would take care of us and provide. I sat for many an hour in the sunshine by the window reading and meditating. He had always provided the necessities. He cared for the sparrow—why not our little family? Nothing was too hard for God.

Early Thanksgiving morning, we got a call from the landlady downstairs that a package had arrived for us marked, "perishable." What was it? Food! It had sliced turkey and other meat along with cheese, tuna fish, and all the expensive goodies that I didn't even buy when I had some money! The Lord had not only provided but over and abundantly. I will never forget that as long as I live!

Then, in February, our first baby arrived. The baby was fine and dandy, but I had a rough delivery and would need to be in the hospital a full ten days and then home in bed for a full week with help. There again, the Lord provided a Christian woman to take care of the baby, and He provided Christian fellowship close by, as a wonderful missionary home opened up right across the street. Through this fellowship with other Christians, the Lord strengthened me both spiritually and physically for the years ahead and the problems I would be encountering as well as the many joys I would share.

I was working in the office in a small store where I had very little pay for the long hours I worked and with a baby a year old. I had to rely on the Lord for strength. A few months later, a government position opened up, and after my interview, I was hired immediately. My salary tripled overnight, and my working hours actually shortened! I was so thankful for what the Lord had done.

One of the gifts the Lord gave me was the gift of energy and a love for children. I taught Sunday School ever since I was a senior in high school. I taught for 35 years in the Junior Department—boys ages 9 to 12, and for several years, I had a Sunday night youth group called "Joys and Jets" for this same age range at Calvary Church in Charlotte. The most important thing in teaching or in anything you do is being faithful. No matter how tired I felt, I was always present. Most of the time, I did not miss more than one or two Sundays in a whole year, except for the time out to bring my babies into the world.

During the Second World War in 1945, my husband never expected he would be called into the service, as he was already at the age limit, and we had one child and were expecting another, but he was drafted and had to go. This was one of the hardest things for him, to turn over to the Lord and just accept the fact that he had to go. During his time in the Army, he was hospitalized twice for minor surgeries, but each time, he missed being sent into a big battle where many of his company were killed, including the Battle of the Bulge. There again, we had much to thank the Lord for. You can believe he had a wife at home constantly praying for him!

During this time, I was expecting my second child, but the Lord did not see fit to allow this child to live. It was stillborn at seven months. Tests were made, and it was found that this child had been dead for six weeks. According to all reports, I should have had blood poisoning, but my blood test came out perfect. Doctors came by in the hospital to look at my records, then they all poked their heads in the door to take a look at me. What did I look like after this unusual birth? Well, I looked just fine, so there again, I had to just praise the Lord.

While my husband was overseas, I spent time in the north with my relatives. Part of this time I spent with my father, who had just lost his second wife. The first Sunday I was there, I attended church. When I was in the women's class, the superintendent came and asked if any woman would volunteer to teach a class of 14-year-old boys. They desperately needed a teacher. He waited a good while, and no one volunteered. Here I was, new in town, and attending this church for the first time, but I felt the Lord wanted me to say yes, if they didn't mind me being a visitor. They said this was just fine, and they were very grateful if I would take the class. My father was well known in town, but he rarely attended church. The boys were so eager to have a teacher and study that they would sit still and hardly move at all. I couldn't believe it! If one interrupted, he would get a quick punch from the boy next to him, and all would get quiet again immediately. I had the privilege of teaching them for six months until I had to move on, but I can truthfully say this was one of the most rewarding and enjoyable periods of my life. They were starving for love and attention and, above all, to hear the Word of God!

After the war years, a girl and three more boys were born to us. The last boy was perfectly formed in every way, but he was a stillborn. Although I had four children, still, I looked forward to this little life. It was one of those unexpected pregnancies. The Lord again tried my faith. We had just moved into a new home, and a few months later, my husband lost his job, and here I was pregnant. Still, I was determined to trust the Lord, even though I didn't understand His plan, but God doesn't always give us the answers. He means for us to trust Him, and this I was determined to do.

About a year later, my husband found out that he had a terminal illness. Again, I had to trust the Lord, even though I didn't understand why we had to go through so many deep waters. However, I always reassured myself and my husband that other families who loved the Lord also had hard things to go through and even harder places. The Lord does not promise that we will have it easy, but He does say He will always be with us!

This was written to help teenagers and young mothers cope with day-to-day circumstances by fully committing themselves to the Lord and being renewed daily.

Kathryn Ritzman Sellers

(Kathryn went on to live to be 96 years old. She outlived two husbands and her youngest son, Bob. She was very instrumental in starting three ministries at Calvary Church, with one continuing to this day. She also raised four children, seeing three of them graduate from college and one of these from graduate school. In addition, she taught Sunday School classes for 35 years. She quit work at the age of 81, then regretted it!)

Chapter 2

Singing Ho for Carolina

From the fourth grade to the twelfth grade and beyond, the place that had a tremendous impact on my life was "Carolina Bible Conference" or "Camp Carolina" near Boone, North Carolina. I can remember riding in the old black camp car, maybe a 1949 Plymouth, up the mountains from Charlotte to Boone. As we rode out of the 90-degree heat and humidity of Charlotte on the way to the beautiful Blue Ridge Mountains, we sang the camp song, "Singing Ho for Carolina." The temperature got cooler and cooler as we sang along, "Singing ho for Carolina, Carolina, Carolina, singing ho for Carolina the best camp around. With a skyrocket and a bombshell and a firecracker and a cowbell, singing ho for Carolina the best camp around."

Carolina Bible Conference was under a loose-knit board of some of the leading men from Calvary Church in Charlotte. My dad, John Alton Sellers, ended up among this group of board members. The property was given by a retired Presbyterian minister who had a large home on the property. We called him Dr. Mack or Pastor Mack. He and his wife started a school for mountain boys back in the old days when there were not a lot of schools available for those who lived deep back in the mountain valleys. They had about 80 acres of land that ran to the top of a small mountain on one side and ran down to a large mountain trout stream on the other side.

To make the camp, Dr. Mack had about 25 boys come and help him build a large dorm that had some staff bedrooms downstairs along with a large bath and shower room, a small living room, and a kitchen

with a good-sized dining room. There was a separate bedroom that ran off the dining room with a bathroom attached for the cook. Across from the main dorm building was an old water mill house right on the river filled with trout and large rocks. This remodeled mill house provided space for classrooms and a chapel.

After Dr. Mack's wife passed away, he closed the school and continued to live in the big house beside the main dorm. He adopted one of the boys who was in the school and helped him get started in independent living. This young man visited Dr. Mack once per week or so to help him get groceries, go to the doctor, etc. Dr. Mack wanted to live in his home until he passed away, but he wanted the rest of the buildings and property to be used for ministry. So, he donated it to a group of men who agreed to form a non-profit Bible Conference with the board that I mentioned from Calvary Church. They called it "Carolina Bible Conference." Later, this property was given to Calvary Church in Charlotte.

For a number of years, Calvary Church used Carolina Bible Conference for Junior Camp (grades 4 to 6), Jr. High Camp (grades 7 to 9), and Senior High Camp (grades 10 to 12). Ma Sample, the director of the Junior Dept. at Calvary Church ran the Junior Camp for about ten years, I think. She brought in students and staff from Southeastern Bible College to help her run the camp. Ma Sample made sure that every one of her students got to camp each summer as long as they wanted to go, and most everyone did. She and her husband would pay for any amount that a student didn't have to make sure they got to camp.

Ma Sample was a very strict person, and she ran a tight ship, so to speak, but she had a heart of gold and cared deeply about all her campers. Every evening during the first day or two of camp, she would go down the row as we lined up for evening meal with a jar of castor oil. She would ask each camper, "Have you had a BM today?" If you said, "No," you got a spoon full of castor oil! I was glad to be near the end of the line so I could see what she was doing. When she got to me, I would say loud and clear, "Yes ma'am, I had two!"

Ma Sample and her husband paid the way for all the campers to go to "Tweetsie Railroad" every year in the middle of the camp week. I will never forget the day that we went to Tweetsie and got on the old steam engine train to take a 40-minute ride around this small mountain. The train stopped twice as it made its way around the mountain. First, there was a robbery when some robbers stopped the train and took a case of money out to steal it. Then the "sheriff" and his men showed up and arrested the robbers and put the money case back on the train and we headed on around the mountain.

After this, the train continued until it was attacked by Indians. The Indians would get on the train and run through from one end to the other. When the last Indian ran through the car that our campers were on, one of our campers pulled out a heavy metal toy gun and clobbered this Indian (a student from Appalachian State University) on the back of his head! This Indian hurried off the train holding his head. He had to go and have several stitches put in at the hospital. We noticed in future years that the Indians never came back on the train again. They just ran around the train on the outside. The "guards" on the train would shoot at them and run them off.

My second year at Camp Carolina I was 12 years old and in the fifth grade. (I had to repeat the second grade because my reading level was too low.) I remember going out to sit on one of the big rocks in the middle of the trout stream – praying and reading my Bible and just taking in the beauty of it all. I enjoyed the sun and listening to the fast-moving water over the rocks all around me as it moved toward the old mill house and on into the calmer waters below.

The last night of camp was a candle-light service. All those who wanted to take a public stand for Jesus and dedicate their lives to following Him were invited to come to the front and light a candle and place it in a holder to represent your commitment. This was my first public witness of my faith in Christ. After I went forward, two of my friends came behind me as well. It made me feel good that I was able to "break the ice" for them. Camp Carolina was a special place. I have so many memories and a deep emotional attachment for this place, and I know that I always will. In many ways, it is my "Bethel."

Back in those days, the buildings were badly in need of remodeling, rewiring, replumbing, and many other repairs. We had to work hard every year to get the state inspector to give us a passing grade for our kitchen. We always had Mary, our cook, make a special homemade apple pie for him. We worked hard cleaning the floors, painting the walls, shining up the sinks, and doing many other chores. I think we usually got a B- or a B grade, a passing grade that we could live with for one more year!

The property had several old apple trees out beside the softball field. We would go out to pick a good number of these old cooking apples. We would bring them to Mary and beg her to make us a good apple pie. She would always play with us and act as if she could not do it, but she always gave in to us, and let me tell you, that was the best apple pie you could ever think about eating—it was to die for!

Then there was the annual raid on the girls' dorm—the main building with the kitchen downstairs and two large halls of rooms upstairs where the girls slept. The boys slept in the upstairs of the old mill house down by the river. They would sneak over to the girls' dorm and try to run up the stairs with buckets of cold water from the stream. The girls would be waiting for them with their own buckets of water and would douse the guys when they got halfway up the stairs. Women staff would bring out the brooms and chase the boys back to their place.

One year, the regular people who ran the Senior High Camp were not able to do it. So, the board leaders talked a 40-some-year-old schoolteacher named Elva into being in charge. She had been warned about the boys raiding the girls' dorm, usually on the last night of camp. Elva waited until the boys had all bunked down in their sleeping bags in the old mill house. She then came and walked up the stairs and turned the light on to make a firm announcement. She told us she was not going to put up with any raids. She stated, "I am going to be watching you and will be back soon to make sure you are all here."

After she left, several boys who had a bunk bed close to the stairs that led up from the first floor decided to pull their pants down and be ready to "moon" Elva the next time she came up. In about an hour, Elva made her way up with a flashlight. She shined the light on their bunk beds to make sure we were all there only to see about four shining bare butts on top of the sleeping bags. "Well, I see you are all here," she said and hurried down the stairs and back to the girls' dorm as the boys were laughing their heads off.

Another camp tradition was we would always take Dr. Mack a meal at least once per day when the camp was in session. I would often be one of those who would take a meal to his room in his big house. He lived out of one large room upstairs with an old coal-burning stove to keep him comfortable. Dr. Mack loved to talk and tried to get you to stay as long as possible. One day he seemed very upset about something. I asked him what he was upset about. He said to me, "Have you ever heard a preacher cuss?" I said, "No." He replied, "Well, if you had been here earlier you would have. I saw a fisherman come in here, and he caught my pet trout. I've been feeding that trout for a long time. This is my property, and he had no business coming in here and catching my pet trout!"

Another time, Dr. Mack was talking about a time when his wife was alive. He said that he would be called on often by people who lived back in the hills to come and do a wedding or a funeral. One time, a person he didn't know at all wanted him to come and do a funeral service. His wife asked him, "Well, Pastor, what are you going to say?" He said, "I told her I was going to say 'Ashes to ashes, dust to dust, if the Lord don't have him, the devil must.' " We all got a laugh out of this, many times over.

On several occasions through the years, I would bring a small group of high-risk kids to the old Camp Carolina property. I had a deep desire for these boys who had rarely, if ever, had any kind of Christian camping experience, to be able to have at least two days and two nights in this beautiful and amazing place of God's creation.

One time, we rented a cabin just up the street from the camp. I came with a recreation director from a juvenile unit and a fellow graduate student from South Africa who was ten times more excited than the boys. Right after we arrived, while we were unloading the van, I heard several of the boys screaming for joy just on the other side of the cabin. I hurried over to that side to see them jumping into the fast-moving trout stream in their jeans and riding the stream down a good distance. Then, they would get out and run back so that they could jump in again. This experience, along with the many times I took high-risk and institutionalized boys on their first fishing trips, brought great joy to my heart just to see them have a chance to be real kids. For so much of their young lives, they had been in the middle of dysfunctional families where they were forced to be the adults in an atmosphere of drug abuse, sexual abuse, and alcoholism.

I thank God for the wonderful camping experiences I had growing up as a young man in a stable Christian home and in a church that gave emphasis on good Bible teaching and good modeling from so many of the male church members. Every time I think back on that, I realize anew how blessed I have been!

Chapter 3

The Miracle of Prayer

Prayer- The Essential Element of Successful Living

There are people out there who are real doubters when it comes to prayer. They believe that things just happen, and if something occurs that we wish for or pray for, it's just a circumstantial happening. I learned early in life that the Lord does answer prayer and seeks to give us the desires of our hearts when our heart is beating in tune with His! I believe in the God of the Bible, who desires to be a personal dad to

His children who put their trust in Him as their personal Lord and Savior. I can believe in this God because many times in my life, I have experienced Him giving direct answers to a personal prayer need and even to personal desires like being able to go to a ball game!

A Big Answer to Getting a Ticket to a Braves Game

I lived in Atlanta for five years. On several occasions, I was able to go with a friend to an Atlanta Braves baseball game. One weekend, I was alone, as all my friends were gone for the weekend. I got this desire to go to a Braves game, so in faith, I took the train to downtown Atlanta and got off at the Capitol station. I walked over to the old Braves stadium hoping to buy a ticket outside the stadium.

The only tickets being sold were $100 and up since the game was sold out. I said to the Lord, "Well, Lord, if you want me at this game, you will have to provide the ticket." I began walking back to the train station, but when I looked ahead, I saw a well-dressed lady in her 40s walking to the stadium by herself. When she got near me, I was led to smile and ask her if she had a ticket for sale. She smiled back and told me she did have an extra ticket. She sold it to me for $15!

This was no big miracle, but the Lord seemed to speak to me in a special way to let me know that He did care about encouraging me, even in the little things, because He knew I needed encouragement in that time in my life.

I'm Dreaming of a White Christmas

When I was a kid, about 14, I and some friends were complaining that we might grow up without ever having a white Christmas. My mom overheard us and said to us, "Have you ever prayed about this?" We looked at each other and said, "Well, no," so we prayed that the Lord would give us a white Christmas. On Christmas Day that year, Charlotte got a good white Christmas! Our parents allowed us to go out in a miraculous moonlit night to the Charlotte Country Club until midnight. I will never forget that Christmas because it was the most memorable of my childhood. Just walking through the woods in the newly fallen snow under a bright moon was extremely exciting. What a joy for a group of 12, 13, and 14-year-old boys.

I am told that Charlotte has only had four white Christmas Days in 139 years. To me, this was a miraculous answer to prayer and just another reason to believe that I serve a God who really does love to answer prayer. God desires to build the faith of His people, and His answer to prayer helped a 14-year-old kid who was learning to trust Him in small things so that I can be prepared to trust Him in much larger things in the years ahead.

The Miracle at Garinger High

I attended Garringer High School on the northeast side of Charlotte. At the time, Garinger had just over 2,000 students and 500 in my senior class.

My junior year, I joined a small YFC/Campus Life Club at my high school. We had about 7 students who met at a home on the edge of the school property once a week with our YFC staff to pray for our school and find ways to share the life-changing message of Jesus with our fellow students.

We decided to have a special outreach using a contest between the two main boys' clubs at the school—the Key Club and the Inter-act Club. We got permission to use the small gym at the school to have an eating contest called "The World's Largest Banana Split!" We got new rain gutters and covered them with aluminum foil. The ice cream and other ingredients were donated. This covered gutter went the whole length of the small gym. The most popular teen radio station picked up on this event and began pushing it several days leading up to this Friday night event. It became the place to go that weekend, and we had more kids show up than we could fit in the gym.

Long story short, it wasn't long after the clubs began the contest that someone began throwing the ice cream and bananas at the team across from them. The floor became so slick that no one could stand up. The teams were falling and getting covered in ice cream, bananas, and whipped cream. They soon left to get cleaned up and never came back, so our plan to share the life-changing message of Jesus after the contest didn't work out. We had gained good advertising for YFC, but we didn't get to share the most important message so many of these guys needed to hear!

I attended a YFC weekend retreat when speakers Willie Foote and Bill Aiken challenged us to trust the Lord to do something impossible in our lives and in our school—something that only He could make happen! I decided I was going to trust the Lord to enable us to reach the whole school with the gospel before I graduated. To me, that was the most impossible thing I could pray for, and I knew that only God could make that happen!

Soon after this commitment, our elective Bible teacher, Janet Robinson, asked me if I would join the Religious Activities Committee, which held a traditional Easter Assembly and Christmas Assembly each year. I accepted the invitation and attended my first committee meeting. In my first meeting, they were in the middle of planning the Easter Assembly. I was told that they had planned the music part with the choir and had secured someone to supply flowers, decide on a date, and other essential decisions. The only thing left to secure was the speaker. They told me that would be my job!

I began to pray that the Lord would give me the wisdom and direction to find the right speaker. I was told that the school was under pressure from the ACLU to do away with these religious assemblies, and this might be the last assembly we would be allowed to have.

On a side note, when my older brother attended this high school, they had both of these religious assemblies every year along with Bible I and Bible II English elective classes and a Monday morning prayer and Bible study time led by the Bible teacher, Miss Robinson, in the auditorium before classes began each week. Several hundred students would attend this weekly event, and the principal thought this was a great way to begin each school week! Today, Garinger High School no longer has Bible classes, religious assemblies, or Monday morning Bible studies. Every week, students are being taken out in handcuffs. It has become one of the worst schools in the state of North Carolina. When I attended there, it was one of the best high schools in the state! Is this the result of our "progressive, politically correct improvements?"

But back when we were still planning the Easter Assembly, I was led by the Lord to think of a former student of the school who had become a minister and a missionary to Ethiopia, Bill Harding. Bill was a former tennis star at the school and a well-known speaker at colleges all over the country. He was a very busy Christian leader, so I called Bill to see if he would be available, somewhat doubting that he would be. I was excited to hear him tell me that he was going to be in town that day and would be glad to come back to his old high school and give the message at the Easter Assembly. I remembered that this might be the last Easter Assembly we would be allowed to have, so I told Bill that I wanted him to give a very clear gospel presentation and the real meaning of Easter.

The day came for the Easter Assembly. The auditorium only held 1,000 people, so we had to have two assemblies to hold all the students who wanted to come (instead of going to study hall). Both assemblies were well attended by students, staff, and teachers. I don't think there were even a handful of students in study hall, if there were any at all. I was nervous since I had to give the opening prayer and introduce the speaker twice! I had never been in front of so many people at one time in my life. This was made worse when I was told by my Bible teacher that she had been told that we should not pray "in Jesus' name!" Then, she winked at me and said, "Just do whatever the Lord leads you to do, John." I didn't know any other way to pray, especially for an Easter Assembly, so I prayed in the name of our Risen Lord Jesus both times!

Our speaker, Bill Harding, did a great job. He related to the students and gave a very clear presentation of why Jesus had to shed His blood on the cross for our sinful fallen nature. Reverend Harding had a group of students who came forward after both assemblies to talk with him. A number were even Jewish students!

As I struggled to move through the packed crowd on the way out of the second assembly, a tall male student reached over and tapped me on the shoulder. When I turned back to face him, he simply said, "Thank you." At that moment, the Holy Spirit spoke to me and said, "Do you realize that today I answered your impossible dream to see your whole school get to hear the gospel before you graduate?"

Every time I think back on that awesome day, I realize that the Lord used that day to let me know that it didn't matter that I wasn't super talented; it didn't matter that I was only 5'7" and 110 lbs. It didn't matter that I wasn't very athletic. What mattered more than anything else was that I believed God to work a miracle and that I was learning to depend completely on Him and trust Him to make it happen. As the Bible states, "Without me, you can do nothing." As Paul reminds us, "I can do all things through Christ who strengthens me." On this day, one of the greatest days of my life, and possibly in the history of Garinger High School, God made mission impossible possible.

I don't know what happened in the life of all 2,000 of those students, but I do know that one of those students, Don Minday, went on to commit his life to the Lord at North Carolina State University through the Navigators and ended up as a lifetime missionary in France. Another student, Jim Nash, found the Lord while playing football for the University of South Carolina and became a leading Christian businessman for many years in Columbia, South Carolina. I also was impacted as I was encouraged to commit my life to full-time service and to serve the Lord through YFC for over 25 years. It will be exciting to get to Heaven and find out how many more of those 2,000 students found Jesus and served Him in various ways throughout their lives.

During my high school years, we tried a lot of crazy things to share Jesus with our lost friends, and though many failed miserably, the Lord taught me the need to wait upon Him to open the right doors and see Him use His Word to draw people to Himself. He did this clearly in the Easter Assembly, and through the years that I have served, I have seen Him connect youth to the gospel through many different doors. Altogether, the Lord has allowed me to present the life-changing message of Jesus to over 8,000 youth. Only Heaven will tell how many of these youth fully received Christ and followed Him.

One day on my way to Charlotte to visit my mom and family, I stopped by Columbia Bible College to have lunch and visit a few of my old professors. When I sat down at a table in the dining room, three male students came and sat down across from me. I introduced myself to them as an alumnus working with Youth for Christ. One of these students asked me if I remembered him. I told him since I have worked with hundreds of young men over the years, he would need to remind me. He said I worked with him when I was with YFC in Raleigh. He said, "You took me on a retreat to the mountains with several other high school kids. I was drinking and doing drugs back then, but now I'm a senior here at CBC and will soon be graduating."

I almost fell out of my chair! What a joy it was for me to have this God-appointed encounter with this young man. I don't know when he decided to follow Jesus, but I know that I had the privilege of sharing the gospel with him on that retreat when I showed him and the other students the movie, *The Cross and the Switchblade.* How gracious the Lord was to allow me to meet this student out of the blue, so to speak, so that I could be encouraged to know that my many years of hard work was not in vain. Yes, there were some who went all the way with Jesus!

Another young man, Neal, called me at 3:00 a.m. I wondered who on earth was calling at that time in the morning, but the Holy Spirit told me it was Neal before I picked it up, and sure enough, it was Neal! Neal apologized for calling me so early, but he said that he wasn't able to sleep. He had been listening to a preacher present the gospel on the radio and felt the speaker was talking to him personally. At the end of the message, Neal said that he prayed to receive Christ as his personal Savior. He had become a believer! After making this commitment, Neal remembered that he had told me, "John, one day, I am going to become a Christian, and you will be the first to know." This was why he had called me at 3 a.m. I will take those calls anytime!

One day, I went to a park in south Charlotte to meditate and pray. I sat on a bench and looked out on the park to see a young dad with his son. As I watched them play gleefully together, the thought came to me, "John, you will never have that joy. You will never get to raise your own son." Tears came to my eyes, but immediately, the Holy Spirit spoke to me and said, "It's not your calling to raise your own son and children, but you will have the joy of ministering and helping raise hundreds of young men who need Jesus. Yours is a higher calling because you will reach more youth than you would ever as a dad." A great peace came over me, and I was able to accept this special calling with the confidence that the Lord was going to make this just as rewarding and just as satisfying as raising my own son or daughter.

Later, I did become a foster dad and was given a foster son. Matt lived with me from the time he was in 9th grade, right up to just before he graduated from high school. He was the only one in his family to graduate from high school.

The Day the Rain Stood Still

When I was vice president of the student association at Columbia Bible College (Columbia International University), I oversaw the recreation day in the spring. This was the weekend the school invited prospective students to come and have a free weekend to check out the college. Several hundred high school students came to spend two nights at the college. They attended classes, a chapel service, and spent two nights in the dorms. On Saturday, we planned several hours of outdoor recreation for these special guests. We had no indoor gym at the time, so it was very important to have good weather on that day.

A few days before the weekend, the weather report came out. It was not at all encouraging. The report called for 100 percent rain that coming Saturday. I told my committee that we had a God who is Lord over the weather, and I knew that He could give us clear weather for this important day. We just needed to trust Him to do that and pray to that end.

On that Saturday, it rained all over Columbia, in about every community, but it did not rain at Columbia Bible College. We had dry weather for the entire two hours, and only later in the day did we get any rain. The Lord made believers out of all of us, especially those who felt that we really need to go with a plan B movie in the chapel.

My Awesome Mailbox Experience during Grad School

During my time at Columbia Bible College, I heard many students talk about "mailbox experiences." They would need a very specific amount of money, and just in time, without anyone really knowing what they needed, they would go to their mailbox, and the exact amount would be sent to them. I would occasionally get a $5 or $10 gift from my mom, but that was the extent of any mailbox experiences, except for when I got "a notice from Otis."

Otis Braswell was the dean of me at the college, and if he caught you breaking a rule or coming in after curfew, he would send you a notice to come and see him. When you got this note, you knew you were going to get a work penalty of some kind or another, yet Mr. Braswell had an amazing way of handing out these penalties in such a way that you felt it was a wonderful learning experience meant to grow your character, emotionally and spiritually.

One summer, I was taking classes in grad school. I had just used all the money I had to pay off my school bill for the summer when I got a call from the mother of a young man that I had worked with extensively for several years. She was in tears as she told me that he was in a bad accident in south Florida near Fort Myers. Neal was not expected to live, but he survived, though paralyzed from the waist down. His mother asked me to please go down and see him as soon as I could to help her get him back up to Charlotte. I promised I would as soon as my classes were over.

No one knew this need, but I prayed the Lord would supply the funds to make the trip down to check on Neal and see if he was ready to follow Jesus as well as get up to Charlotte where he could get better care. Neal had been hit by a church van while he was riding a bike back from a convenience store in Fort Myers. He was thrown a good distance in the air and landed on his spine.

About two weeks after talking with Neal's mom, I went to get my mail and noticed that there was a letter in my box from a lady in Charlotte whose family owned a department store. I had not heard from her in over 3 years. She never sent me more than $100, but this letter included a check for $300! This was just the amount I needed to make the trip to Florida. Ann Eliza Tate was used by the Lord to answer a need that she knew nothing about, but more than that, the Lord used her to build my faith and enable me to grow in my understanding that if the Lord calls you, He will supply what you need to fulfill that calling. He has done that my entire life. Great is His faithfulness. Just as my mom always taught us, "The Lord will work it out!"

My Amazing Trip to Israel

For many years, I had a deep desire to go to Israel. When I was taking Bible I in high school, my Bible teacher, Janet Robinson, shared pictures and stories with us of her trip to Israel. This was the start of my growing desire to see Israel myself.

When I was in my last year of grad school in 1987, I felt the Holy Spirit leading me to step out in faith and believe God that the time was right to go to Israel. I found out that if I signed up my last year of grad school, I could get a discounted student rate of $1,600 for a three-week study tour that covered all costs, including travel and all meals, fees, and lodging. I trusted the Lord to provide the funds and paid a $200 deposit.

During the Christmas break of my last year of grad school, the head of the cafeteria, Bill Level, asked me if I could come back the day after Christmas and wash dishes for a special conference that was going to be held over the Christmas break at the University. He said he would give me $600. I took this as an answer to my prayer that God would provide the remaining $1,400 for Israel! That brought my balance down to $800.

I told my family that I didn't want any gifts for Christmas, instead, if they wanted to give me a gift, they could give me money toward the trip. I think I got $200 from my family that year for Christmas; now I only needed $600 more. I was able to get a $500 credit loan from the bank with the gifts I got from graduating. Through other small blessings, I had $200 in spending money to take with me on the trip!

The miracle trip to Israel continued when I arrived at the airport in New York. When I got off the shuttle bus at the terminal, I needed to meet my fellow students headed to Israel inside. When I saw a group of these students, I joined them and set my bags down. It was then that I realized there was one very important case I didn't have. I had made a terrible mistake: my attaché case was still on the shuttle bus! That case held my travel money, passport, and my return plane tickets. Without my passport, my trip to Israel was gone.

I asked my friends to watch my bags and pray. I rushed out and went into the next shuttle bus to tell the driver what I had left in one of the shuttle buses. He told me that I could check his bus and the other four buses that would be coming behind him, but he said, "I hope you find it, but this is New York. I wouldn't count on it." I went into three more buses as they came in, but my case was not on any of them.

There was only one bus left, and I was trying as hard as I could to believe God, but my heart was starting to sink in my chest. Finally, the last bus rolled in and some people filed out. I told the driver what I was looking for, and he told me I was free to look. I walked to the back of the bus where I was sitting, and there was my attaché case. It was not locked, but when I opened it, everything was still in there, including my $200.

I thanked the bus driver as I left rejoicing. He looked at me and said, "That is a miracle!" I had to agree. "Thank you, Lord! Thank you, thank you, thank you!"

My Guardian Angel in Atlanta

I lived in Atlanta for five years from about 1990 to 1996. I was working as a part-time juvenile chaplain at Lorenzo Benn Youth Development Center, overseeing juvenile institutional assemblies using multi-media and helping Presbyterian Evangelistic Fellowship start a juvenile halfway house. I was working hard, but I had very little support coming in.

Late one afternoon, I was in the middle of moving from a small bachelor's apartment to a condo. I was entering the interstate in downtown Atlanta, which was one of the worst crime areas. I looked ahead to the onramp after looking left to merge when I saw a large chunk of cement, which some construction truck had apparently dropped, in the middle of the ramp. I couldn't miss it, but I was able to steer around it on my front side, where it hit my back tire and popped it. I was able to go back onto an offramp and stop.

When I got out of my truck and looked under the rear, I realized that I didn't have the key with me to get into my spare tire. I also realized a dark cloud was moving west toward me. This was not looking good at all. It was after 5 p.m. and would soon be getting dark.

Suddenly, I looked up and to the right of my truck stood a young black man in a white shirt. I didn't see him approaching and had no idea where he came from, but suddenly, he was there saying, "Can I help you?" I told him my problem, and he told me he had a friend who was a locksmith. I felt led to go with this young man, and on the way to the locksmith, he told me he was in a church choir.

The locksmith was still in his office and was willing to come and get my spare tire out. He did a fast job and even put my tire on for me. I gave him the $15 I had in my wallet and told him I would send him more money if he would give me his address. He was fine with what I gave him, and soon, I was on my way. I had heard other people talk of guardian angel experiences, but this was the first time in my life that I really felt like the Lord sent an angel to my rescue.

Several years before this, I had been mugged by a young black man very close in age to this young man who had assisted me. The Lord knew I needed this experience to help me build faith in the black community again. This was a real growing experience for me, and I will always look back on it with great appreciation both to the Lord and to the portion of the black community in inner city Atlanta. They showed me a heart of concern for someone in need, regardless of color.

The Ultimate Rescue

During my trip to Israel, we made a trip to the Mediterranean Sea one day, and on the way back, we stopped to look at some caves that had been used for Jewish burial sites. The first cave was much like an open room that you walked straight into from a carved opening that they would often roll large stones over, much like they did with Jesus. Inside was several burial sites on both sides, with a large site at the end for the patriarch of the family. Underneath the site for the patriarch was a large hollow space. This, we were told, is where the bones of the others buried there with him would be thrown about a year after their burial. This is what it means in the Bible when it says, "the bones were gathered to their fathers."

Across from this first cave was another large cave. This one had a tunnel that you had to crawl through single file before it opened into a decently sized cave. We were told by our guide that if we didn't want to crawl through the tunnel, we could climb on top of the cave and look in from the outside where there was a large hole.

I, along with an 85-year-old and 90-year-old from our group, climbed up on top to look in from the edge of the hole. When one of our nurses decide that she wanted to go down and crawl through the tunnel, she started walking in front of me close to the edge of the drop off. I didn't want her so close to the edge, so I stepped back about two yards only to find out there was a small hole directly behind me that also emptied into that cave.

I fell feet first about ten feet, then hit a small ledge and flipped, falling headfirst into the cave full of people who didn't know I was coming. My right arm went out to protect my head, and I crushed my right wrist in four places. I also cracked my left wrist slightly and had a gash on my lip and forehead that needed stitches. I was knocked out for several seconds, and when I woke up, one of the nurses was talking to me. I had just fallen 15 feet into this cave, but I was glad I hadn't broken my leg.

I soon realized that I had destroyed my right wrist and knew this was going to be a challenge. Luckily, the Israeli military were on the scene within ten minutes. They told me, "Do not move. We are going to drag you out." One of the soldiers was in front and one in back as they dragged me out by my pants through the tunnel. Even though a military ambulance had come, the officer in charge decided I was okay to go to the hospital by way of our tour bus. I sat in the back of the bus with the two nurses tending to me while our Arab bus driver sped to Jerusalem yelling, "Out of the way. Emergency, emergency. Out of the way."

I spent the night in the main hospital in Jerusalem with doctors and nurses trying to talk to me in Hebrew. I had to tell them over and over that I didn't speak Hebrew. I think my dark hair and big nose made them think I was Jewish! I was seen by three doctors, had my right wrist and arm put in a cast, had stitches in my forehead and mouth, and was checked for internal bleeding. This, along with spending the night in the hospital came to a grand total of about 350 American dollars. My group took up a collection to pay for this bill.

When some of the staff where we were staying were told of how God had saved my life and brought me out of a cave the way Jesus had brought Lazarus back from the dead, I was told several of them prayed to receive Christ! This was happy news, and I felt that if my experience was what led them to Christ, then I was happy to go through it all. I stayed for another full week and took a medical flight home to get a special operation on my right wrist in Charlotte.

What started out as $350 in Israel turned into over $6,000 in the US! My student insurance only paid half of this. I had to make a hard decision not to file a lawsuit to get the remaining $3,000 because I felt the Israeli guide was negligent in not scouting out the area before sending us up there, but these are life lessons that we all go through at times. I was glad it was me that fell and not the two elderly with me. I felt the Lord had saved me for a reason, and He had a purpose and a calling for me.

I later found my calling after I had failed over and over to get accepted by men. My answer to the call to come to Iowa and work with Youth for Christ in Iowa City was a beginning of a new life for me that enabled me to get to the State Training School in Eldora, Iowa. This was the place where the Lord allowed me to fully blossom and develop my gifts. Yes, it took a lot of "falls" along the way, but the Lord showed me that when I let Him have full control and take me where He wanted me to be, that was the very best place—Iowa!

Chapter 4

Responding to Rejection: Another Key to Successful Living

I think one thing that has helped me work with troubled youth maybe more than any other thing is the fact that I have been through so many experiences with rejection. I am sure some of this rejection I brought upon myself by making bad choices and decisions that were based on emotions and emotional reactions, but many of these experiences had little to do with my actions. What part I did play was my reaction to the actions of others.

I have been rejected for being too small. I was 110 pounds from junior high school through college. About the only time my small size seemed to lean in my favor was when my high school wrestling team needed someone my size. I was begged to join the wrestling team, and I should have, but my self-image was low at that time in my life, and I struggled with self-confidence.

I was labeled by some as being gay, simply because I was so small and didn't have any girls who were anxious to date me. I had some girls who were close friends, but they were just friends. At one time, a leader that I worked under in Youth for Christ told another staff person that he thought I was gay because I hadn't dated anyone for two years. At that point in my life, I didn't have the funds to take care of my basic needs, much less take someone on a date! I was driving around on bald tires and learning to eat beans and rice.

Another boy in my youth group who was a year younger than I, but much more popular and a very well-built soccer player, asked me to strip down like him before climbing into a queen bed with him when we were on a church trip to New York. Assigning students of the same sex to share a bed on youth retreats was quite common back in those days, and no one thought anything of it. However, this young man was only wearing a small pair of underwear, and he implied that he "could keep me warm" if I didn't put my pajamas on. It was a cold night, and I just joked it off and put on my pajamas and climbed into my side of the bed.

Later, he told other boys in the youth group that I was gay, so he didn't want to share a bed with me on another trip. I was very tempted to tell these boys the truth as I was extremely angry with him. I knew it might lead to a fight, so I let it go and found another place to sleep. However, this boy passed his lie on to his dad, who began joking with me about being gay. I must say this was very hurtful, even though I knew his dad didn't believe it. I just wanted to be accepted as any other boy in the group, and I had no control over the size of my body or whether a girl was interested in me.

Even before this, the neighborhood bully, Nelson, zeroed in on me when I was six years old and was regularly putting me down and making fun of my size and unathletic body. He began calling me "Joanie" on a regular basis in front of the other boys in the neighborhood. I would like to say that this didn't bother me or affect my self-image, but I know that it did make it more difficult for me to feel accepted and even to accept myself.

I noticed in the second grade that I struggled to read the eye chart from a far distance. I didn't want to fail the eye test, and I didn't want glasses because that would make me different from my other friends. So, I got permission to sit near the front of the class right in front of the eye chart. I memorized the eye chart so I could pass the test and didn't get classes until the fifth grade. This hindered my reading and caused me to repeat the second grade. When my dad took me to get glasses in fifth grade, I walked out of the place with new glasses and discovered trees had leaves, individual leaves! Life started to come into perspective, and I began my battle to catch up with my studies.

By the grace of God, and through very hard work, I graduated from high school with honors and was inducted into the National Honor Society. However, even this important day didn't go well, as the new science teacher skipped over my name when she was calling out the students to go to the second assembly to be inducted. I was too scared to ask her to look back over the list and check to see if my name was there, so I was not there to get robed by one of the prettiest beauty queens in the school. When a fellow student returned to class after the assembly to let me know that I did get inducted, this teacher turned beet red and felt terrible. I lied and said it was okay.

I am not sharing these experiences so that my reader can feel sorry for me but so all of us can better understand how rejection can be painful and can shape us and cause us to have very poor self-images and low self-confidence. I have learned over the years, more and more, that what Satan may cause to come to us for evil and discouragement, God can and does turn around for our good. It can make us stronger and prepare us for the many difficulties that we will face the rest of our lives.

One of the most powerful rejections that I underwent early in my career was when I was getting ready to graduate from undergrad school and find a church job to start applying what I had worked so hard to learn during the previous four years at Columbia Bible College. I had served as vice president of the student association and was able to get a pastor friend of mine a chance to come and speak at one of the daily chapel services. This was soon after my dad had passed away in February of my senior year.

My pastor friend came and spoke at the chapel and took me out to eat after the service. He asked me what I was going to do after graduation. I told him that I was looking for a church to work in and get experience with either junior or senior high youth, along with a summer camp program. He told me he needed someone to come and work with a growing junior high youth group and asked me to come by his office after graduation so we could talk about it.

I was very excited and couldn't wait to go and see him. After returning home, I made an appointment with him. He offered me the job to lead the junior high youth program and told me to begin writing down my ideas while I was on vacation with my mom in Pennsylvania. On vacation, I was on cloud nine and couldn't wait to get back to go over my ideas and get his and the present youth leader's feedback.

When I returned, I hurried to the mountains of North Carolina where the present youth director was with youth in the church. I wanted to run my ideas by her before I met with the pastor. As I was speaking to her, she got a very disturbed look on her face. I asked her what was wrong, and she said, "John, I shouldn't be the person to tell you this, but the pastor hired another person for that job while you were gone."

This was extremely painful and one of the lowest points in my life. Soon, I began to think this was God redirecting me to another job. Before this, I had actually been offered a youth position at a smaller Presbyterian Church in Charlotte. I went by to see the pastor at this church only to be told that he had already hired another when I told him I had accepted the job at the bigger church. This was understandable, as I was clearly offered the job and certainly remembered accepting the job with the understanding that it would need to be approved by the elders.

I went back to meet with the pastor who had hired and fired me before I was able to work one day. I was not given a good reason, but when I asked him if he could recommend me to another church, he told me that he would still like me to come and work as his assistant and also have a ministry with the college and career group that was also growing and in need of a teacher and leader. In the end, I was the janitor and office worker along with heading up the college and career group, as this was the only job the elders were willing to give money toward at that time.

It was not long before I found out this pastor was not getting along well with the elders and deacons, and within two years of beginning his ministry there, he walked out without any warning at the end of his last sermon. This was not the way I wanted to begin my career, so I went to a faith-based counselor about it. He asked me, "John, are you sure that you have learned everything that the Lord is seeking to teach you through this? If not, I would encourage you to stay on and not leave until the time is right." This wasn't what I wanted to hear, but in my heart, I felt he was giving me the right advice, so I stayed for another year. I had a very good year with the college and career group. We began a weekly ministry at a local co-ed training school, which went very well. We also had an outreach retreat on a weekend in the mountains where two of the attenders, one gal and a guy, received the Lord as their personal Savior!

I then applied to Youth for Christ and was accepted as an intern the next year. That led to 30 years of ministry with high-risk kids and families. I know now that I grew a lot during that year as a janitor/office worker and college and career leader. As it has been said, "No pain, no gain!" I must say, the pain was real, and I was tempted to be resentful of the person who was given my job behind by back, and I had to learn to overcome jealousy.

I was working for a short while with Presbyterian Evangelistic Fellowship in Atlanta, Georgia, in the late 80s and early 90s. I was offered a position as a chaplain in one of the main male juvenile correction units just west of Atlanta: Lorenzo Benn Youth Development Center. The chaplaincy position had recently been cut from the state budget, so the only thing they had to offer me was a nice front office and a small monthly travel allowance. The rest of my support I had to raise myself, but there was a great potential to build a very solid ministry, as the lady who hired me was open to ideas and supportive.

About the second week at this position, a somewhat large African American lady, who was a cottage director, asked if she could meet with me and another lady who worked with her in the basement of the administration building. At the beginning of the meeting, she made this statement, "We have had a white honky chaplain here for 22 years, and we told them not to give us another one. And now we have you! We just wanted to let you know not to plan on getting any assistance from us."

I had never faced any kind of statement like that before, but I knew right away that I needed an answer from the Holy Spirit, not from my emotions. I said a little prayer and trusted the Lord to give me the right answer. "Well," I said, "right now, I am the only chaplain you have, so how can I address your concerns." She went on to tell me that they endured drab, white services, yet the staff and most of the students are black. They wanted a real church—an Afro-American service. I understood what she meant, so I told her, "Let me see what I can do about that." I think she was a bit taken aback by my willingness to take her seriously and try to address her problems.

It took me several months to find a dependable black church that could come once a month consistently and start and end on time, but I kept praying and searching until the Lord led me to the right church. The church I found was the same church Evander Holifield attended. They came the last Sunday of each month and brought their pastor and their choir.

This church also gave me two black volunteers to come each Tuesday night to lead a Bible study in one of our dorms. They were very dependable and great to work with. I had two more black men who came along with another white volunteer twice each week to lead a faith-based weightlifting club.

By the time I left Lorenzo Benn several years later, they had more black volunteers than ever before, and the staff lady who was against me at the beginning was one of my best friends! I learned a big lesson on how to respond to people and how to depend on the Lord to bring the answers needed. Praise be to God!

I could go on with more stories on rejection, but I will end with one that others could probably identify with in one way or another.

I was elected yearbook editor in college in 1971. Looking back on this, I would have been wiser to give the job to the female student who was running against me and, instead, volunteer to work on her staff and assist, but I took the job without any experience and had to learn as I went. I worked many long hours, often starting at 9:30 p.m. after finishing my other college assignments. I would work until 12:30 a.m. and get up at 6:15 a.m. to start another long day. We had a very low budget and had to depend on volunteers to take and develop pictures and take leadership over the different sections of the book.

It was hard to get all the staff pictures, but we finally got them done. Then, the person in charge of developing these pictures told me that, somehow, they got the wrong solution in the tray and lost all the pictures! We had to go back and retake them, and we were running close to the deadline. In the end, a few of the pictures in the book came out a bit blurry.

After the book was all finished, we included a poetry section in the back and a dedication to two staff ladies who were retiring that year. I was relieved the huge job was finally completed and it wasn't too bad overall, but when I met the president of the college and asked him what he thought of it, his only comment to me was, "too many bad pictures." That was it. He gave no word on the good sections of the book and no word of thanks for all the hours that I had given with no compensation. It was overwhelming to me, and I didn't know how to answer him.

As we all go through life, there are going to be times like these when we work very hard at one job or another and find that we are not appreciated. Yet, I know that if I am working as unto the Lord, I can hear Him say, "Well done. I know you did your best with what you were given." With this, I can keep going, learn from my mistakes and bad choices, and keep seeking to fulfill His will for my life.

When I left my position at the State Training School in Eldora after over 11 years of service, I was expecting the normal staff reception with a few words of thanks from the director and all the usual congratulations. However, when I showed up in the chapel for the farewell reception, I was surprised to see that they were bringing all the students in along with all the teachers and staff. They sat me down on the front row with my wife and began a program that included a group of staff and students dressed in black robes singing a Negro spiritual and swaying back and forth. A good group of Youth for Christ staff were in attendance as well. Several students were chosen to give a personal thank you to me, and I was given a big stack of thank you letters from staff and students as well as a basketball signed by many of the staff and students. It was such a wonderful surprise, and I was so thankful that the Lord had given me this special place to serve and to have such an overwhelming appreciation for what the Lord had allowed me to accomplish. Praise ιι _ to God!

A few other positions also gave me nice farewells, such as when I left my last part-time chaplaincy job at a small juvenile unit in Columbia, I was given a nice farewell lunch and have been told several times by the director how much I am missed and how much they would like to have me back. In addition, that unit has worked hard to continue some of the things I started there. The feelings I have deep in my soul when I am shown love, acceptance, and appreciation are so opposite from the hurt that comes when I have been rejected or told that I wasn't wanted.

After failing to secure a ministry position about seven times in a row, I remember driving down Interstate 40 in Raleigh and crying out to God and asking Him to just give me cancer and take me home because I was so tired of failing and being rejected. When a troubled teen is told, "You are never going to become anything," or "You are a loser," it becomes a discouragement for them. One young man I worked with was told by his counselor before he left a juvenile institution in Columbia, "You won't last 60 days before you reoffend and come back again." This young man's problem, according to the counselor, was his relationship with Jesus and his dependence on Him to give the power to say, "no," and not sexually offend anyone in the future. He was told, "God has nothing to do with whether you reoffend or not."

This young man, Richard, told me that he was going to prove her wrong if it was the last thing he did. I told him, "If that is one of the things that will motivate you, then go for it." He did, and as far as I know, he has never been arrested again. He entered the Navy, married a Navy gal, had two children, and is seeking a career in the Navy. I was able to visit Richard in Jacksonville, Florida, and took a tour of his ship, met his wife, and saw his home that he was working on fixing up.

Words are powerful and can do tremendous emotional and psychological damage. Often, this comes from those who jump to conclusions at an emotionally intense time. It is almost impossible to take words back as they become implanted in the brain. For example, studies published in *Science Magazine* by researchers from Purdue University and the University of California, Los Angeles, in 2003 demonstrated

cially shunned or turned down by others activates the same
~~ur~~ brains that are associated with experiencing physical pain.
successive studies have corroborated with the similarities
~~ection~~ and physical pain. The article goes on to tell us that
pain is not the only negative consequence of rejection. It can also lead
us to feel more insecure in ourselves, our decisions, and our choices.
Security is one of the most basic human needs, and when it is not met
or is jeopardized by rejections, we start to doubt ourselves.

We also learn there are people with higher senses of self-worth, as
well as individuals with more social power who handle rejection better
than those with lower self-esteem and less influence. Self-confident
people can use rejection to improve themselves, get more creative, and
validate their beliefs.

Rejection will happen to everyone. In time, we can often see that
a rejection was a good thing for us, even when at the time it didn't feel
good and is not easy to understand. Developing more effective responses
to rejection is an important life skill. If we find ourselves unable to deal
with rejection, we may need to work on building our self-confidence and
self-esteem, along with strengthening our social ties before addressing
the anxiety, anger, and other issues that may arise from being rejected.

Bev Flaxington gives us four key steps to deal with rejection:

One- Self-confidence is key

Many people have grown up in environments where they were
told they were worthless or useless. These messages can carry over into
adulthood and other relationships. If your self-confidence is low, start
to build it back. Make a list every day of two or three things you have
done well or contributions you have made to better others. Write these
down and review them before you go to bed each night and again in the
morning. This will fill your night and early morning with something
positive about yourself.

Two- Change to positive self-talk

Don't say thoughts like, "It's all my fault," "What is wrong with
me," or "I'm so stupid." Notice what you are saying to yourself and

choose to build yourself up and concentrate on the positive. The cup can be half full every day and some days even close to full.

Three- Remember, this too shall pass

No one is defined by one bad experience. Don't let one disappointment diminish the worth of everything else that you have experienced.

Four- Practice reframing

Take a deep breath, step back from the situation, and begin to reframe the experience instead of making the situation worse than it is and frame it as an eternal negative. Reframe it by thinking, *"Relationships are hard for everyone. This is hard for me, but I can learn something from it. Let me focus on what I can learn and, if need be, what I can improve on."*

The main things I hope my readers take away from this chapter is the following:

1. Words are powerful. Make sure you have all your facts correct before you come to a conclusion. Remember that most of the time giving grace and mercy will get you further than being right.

2. Know that what Satan intends for evil, the Lord can turn for good. God is not handcuffed by any bad choice that we make or any rejection that we get from others!

3. Treat others as you would want to be treated.

4. Forgiveness is the most powerful force that God has given us. Use it often.

Chapter 5

The Hospital Visit That Broke My Heart

I was running a small halfway house in Charlotte, North Carolina under Youth for Christ in the late 70s. We had helped one of our residents get married to a beautiful young gal that he had a baby with and was expecting another. The couple was living at the halfway house until they could get a place of their own.

I left Jack and Dianne at the house with their 2-year-old son, Bryan, when I left for a weekend conference with Youth for Christ staff in the region. No one else was at the halfway house that weekend. When I returned to the house Sunday afternoon, I saw a note on the door that told me Jack and Dianne had taken Bryan to the hospital. I hurried to the emergency room and asked for them upon arriving at the hospital. The nurse told me the doctor wanted to see me before I went to see Bryan and the family.

I met with the doctor in a private room. He told me he could not accept the story that Bryan's parents were telling him concerning Bryan's head injuries because the head injuries were too extensive and could not have come from falling off the bed. The doctor told me he was going to report this to the Department of Social Services, but he asked if I would closely supervise things if he released Bryan to them in the meantime. I told him I would do my best.

After this visit, I went to see Bryan. My heart sank into my stomach when I saw little Bryan's head. He looked like he had been in a boxing match with a professional boxer! His head and eyes were swollen and was black and blue all over. It was unbelievable; I couldn't imagine that a child's own father would ever do this to him. Bryan was still in diapers! I became suddenly angry at the thought the state system would allow Bryan to go home while an investigation and a decision were made on what was the best placement for Bryan's safety and best interest.

The best I could make out of the situation was that Jack had started drinking and had a drunken confrontation with little Bryan. By the time it was over, Jack had beaten him and left him in this swollen, black and blue state. From then on, I kept a very close watch on Bryan and his parents. It was a week or more before we got a visit from Social Services, but by this time, Bryan's injuries had mostly healed so you could not tell how badly he was hurt by looking at him.

Not long after this, Jack and Dianne moved into their own place and had another two children. Before they left, I noticed that Bryan would not go to his dad. He would come to me and allow me to hold him, and he would peek his head into my office to see if I would let him come in and sit on my lap while I worked at my desk.

As was true of a number of young men I worked with, Jack felt he was God's gift to women. Even though he was married, he continued to play the field. He would drive his wife to work, then go and pick up another woman. He would take her to his house while he was "supervising" his kids. There were times when he did not have the money to keep the house heated or pay other essential bills. He worked here and there but did not get consistent work.

In the end, Bryan was adopted by his mother's parents, who raised hm into adulthood. The other two kids were taken by their mom's sister. I had met Bryan's grandparents several times and knew they were dedicated Christians. Their home property was right beside the little Baptist church they attended.

One day after Bryan had gone to live with his grandparents, I was heading up I-80 near their home and decided to ride by and see how

Bryan was doing. His grandmother welcomed me in and told me that Bryan was doing well. She said he went to church with them every Sunday. One Sunday, Bryan had gone forward at the altar call, and when he came back to his seat, she asked him what he did. Bryan told her, "I was praying." When his grandmother asked him who he was praying for, he said, "I was praying for everybody."

She also told me that recently she was outside working with her flowers with Bryan on the other side of the yard. She heard him talking quite loudly and wondered who he was talking to. When she turned in his direction, she saw him standing on an old tree stump preaching and saying as much as he could remember from the past Sunday's sermon. I told her I hope to hear about his becoming a preacher down the road. I haven't heard yet what became of Bryan.

Looking back, I can say that I learned a lot about our basic sin nature from Bryan's story. God showed me more than ever before what the world, the flesh, and the devil can lead us into and what great consequences we can suffer. Yet, as the life of David in the Old Testament teaches us, the grace and mercy of God can take what Satan intended for evil and turn it for good in the end.

I thank God that He so often enables us to be overcomers so He can prove to us and the watching world His power. He is not bound by Satan. To God be the glory!

Chapter 6

Cell Block Two—Death Row

On Friday, July 1st, 1983, I drove to the old central prison in downtown Columbia, South Carolina. I was going to visit James Terry Roach. Terry Roach was one of the youngest people to ever be sent to death row in South Carolina—16 years of age. He was tried as an adult.

I had worked with Terry when he was at the John G. Richards long-term juvenile training school in Columbia. Terry was a young man with a low IQ level and was easily influenced by other negative teens. When Terry was about one or two months away from being released from his time at John G., his counselor approved for him to attend a weekend faith-based retreat at a local Christian camp. I oversaw this special weekend experience.

We took about 8 boys from John G. to Bethel Bible Camp, a small camp on the east side of Columbia. These boys were able to play football and basketball, go swimming, and have some good food. They also attended several group meetings where a young man shared through music and his personal testimony about being delivered from the darkness of drugs and depression into the light and liberty of the life-changing power of Jesus! Terry and other young men were given the opportunity to give their lives to Jesus and begin a new life in Him before they went back into their home communities. I asked Terry on Friday night after the meeting if he was ready to accept what Jesus did for him and become a believer. Terry said, "I'm not ready yet." Looking back, I now realize how that was the worst decision he made because in just a few short weeks, he would be arrested for rape and murder.

On Saturday afternoon, some boys snuck off the camp campus to a little convenience store where they secured some pot and alcohol. They snuck it back to camp and shared it with Terry. That afternoon, Terry came to me and said, "Some of the guys here are thinking that I'm going to run. Do you think I'm going to run?" I told Terry he was scheduled to go home soon, and I felt he was too smart to run now. He seemed to like my answer, but he and another student did run in the middle of the night Saturday.

Terry was a drug-oriented kid, and he couldn't wait to get some more drugs. He and the other kid ran to a mobile home park where they had been told there was a drug dealer named Shaw. Shaw was about 27 years old and had been kicked out of the service at Fort Jackson due to drugs. Terry's friend must have realized the danger because he left Shaw's place and headed home, but Terry moved in with Shaw and came under Shaw's control, much like a member in Charles Manson's group. Shaw gave Terry alcohol along with drugs through his veins and mouth. Terry told me later that he was drugged out of his mind for about all 30 of the days he was with Shaw.

Shaw took Terry and another guy out twice to find someone to rape. First, they ran a lady off the road in a rural area and raped and killed her. On another night, about two weeks later, Shaw took his gang to a state park on the north side of Columbia. They found a young girl and her boyfriend in a car making out. Shaw pulled out a gun and shot and killed the boyfriend. He then forced Terry and the guy to join with him in raping the girl multiple times. After this, Shaw shot her in the head while she begged for her life. Terry told me when I visited him in jail that Shaw implied that he would shoot Terry as well if he did not participate.

When this came out in the local paper, I was devasted. Obviously, the whole community of greater Columbia wanted quick justice, and most folks felt that the only justice was the death penalty. The other man involved cooperated with the state as a witness and told all the details of what happened. He was given a life sentence without parole. Shaw and Terry were both given the death penalty. Shaw was executed in the electric chair at the new central prison about ten years after his trial. Terry was executed in January 1986 about a year after Shaw.

I always believed Terry should not be executed due to his age at the time, his low IQ, and the fact Shaw seemed to be the one calling the shots and holding the gun. Shaw was also the one who was encouraging Terry to take multiple drugs and alcohol so that he was drugged out of his mind. At the time of these crimes, Terry was about 16 years old.

I was in grad school in Columbia the day Terry was executed. It was a very sad day for me. I had visited Terry four times while he was on death row and one time when he was in jail after he had been arrested. I was told that when the head chaplain at the prison heard that I was in favor of the death penalty for Shaw, I was no longer allowed to visit Terry.

When I did visit Terry at the old Central Prison in downtown Columbia, it was a pretty scary experience! I am a pretty short person, and back then, I was about 110 pounds. After checking into the front desk of the prison, I was sent through several locked gates that emptied me into a long and wide main hall that ran from one end of the prison to the other. This hallway was filled with prisoners with a guard stand spaced along the way about every 50 yards or so. A good distance down this main hallway, there was the door on the right marked "Cell Block Two," which was the death row section. I would knock on the door, and a guard would come to ask my name and let me inside.

There was a two-story row of individual cells where the death row inmates were housed. They were only let out individually one hour a week into a secure recreation area. The rest of the time, they were in their cells unless they had a visitor. This explains why Terry was so happy when I came to visit him. He always had a wide smile and an air of excitement.

On my first visit with Terry in Central Prison, he was brought out to a private room near the front of the prison where I met with him. A guard was always nearby. Because he could not read and write well, when I met with him, we would work a bit on his reading skills and do some Bible reading. My theme with him was to help him "be prepared to live and ready to die." During his time in jail, Terry prayed to accept the Lord as his Savior and was very sorry for his part in all that happened.

The other three visits I had with Terry were at CB-2. There was a small pillbox room with one door and no windows at the very end of this area. The guard would send me into this little room where I would wait for Terry to come in. He would be alone with a big smile from ear to ear. I don't think Terry got many visits, and I know his dad passed away while he was on death row. Obviously, Terry was not able to go to his dad's funeral, and that greatly saddened him.

I went to see Terry at the old Central Prison on Friday, July 1st, 1983, about three years before he was executed. I wanted to spend some time interviewing Terry to better understand his family background and to clarify what happened in his early years to contribute to his criminal behavior.

That day, Terry was in good spirits. We talked about some new security rules, I think this was right after another inmate on death row had committed suicide. That young man had also been from a juvenile unit before he turned 18; he was the one who used to run the video camera during chapel services at the juvenile chapel so that the service could be aired in the lock-up unit. When I heard he had taken his life, it made me wish I had tried to meet with him when I went to see Terry. It caused me to dedicate myself all the more to trying to reach as many institutionalized youth with the life-changing message of Jesus as possible, as long as the Lord would allow me to do it!

I don't remember for sure, but I think it was D. L. Moody who prayed, "Lord, save the elect and then elect some more to be saved!" We know from Scripture that "God is not willing that any should perish, but that all should repent." The Holy Spirit is calling out to many as He was calling out to Terry Roach that night at camp, and if you don't know Him as your Lord and Savior, He is calling out to you to repent and believe that what Christ did on the cross, He did for you. My prayer is that you and others will not say as Terry did, "I'm not ready yet." I know if Terry had a chance to live that night over again, he would have made a different choice.

On my last visit to Terry, I was able to interview Terry to find out more about his life and see what it was that influenced him to go in such a bad direction. Terry shared the following with me, but we began by reading Romans 8:1, Romans 8:28, and 29, and we prayed together that the Lord would help him to be ready to live and prepared to die, according to the will of the governor of South Carolina. The following is an account of Terry's life.

At age 12, when he was in junior high, Terry's friends introduced him to pot, pills, beer, THC, and LSD. In 10th grade, he used acid and cocaine at a concert; he said this was behind his parents' backs. At age 14, his dad caught him with pot. He said his dad put him on a restriction for a month, but he said, "I played my mom against my dad to get what I wanted." At age 15, Terry said he was heavily hooked on drugs.

At age 16, despite his behavior, his dad gave him a 1969 Rambler! He left school and did pot and drugs with his friends. He said, "Other boys and I got drunk, and they suggested that we break into a house. I was sent to the Juvenile Reception and Evaluation Center, but I was still able to get pot there, too." Terry went on to state, "I went back home and fell in love with a girl who came to live at my house, but she was soon taken to a foster home in Greenville, South Carolina."

I asked Terry what his parents were like. He said, "We had a good relationship because they let me do what I wanted, but I needed them to be stricter on me."

Terry then talked about his academics. He said it was hard for him because he was behind and couldn't do the work. "I started out pretty good, but when I was about 7 or 8, my grandfather died. I cried and started having nightmares. When my parents fought, I got upset. My parents would walk out on each other for 2 or 3 days." When Terry was 9 or 10, the school wanted him to attend a special class. He admitted that he stuttered a lot, which caused people to make fun of him; he got into fights with his bullies.

Terry shared of the first time he left home. He was in the 9th grade. "I had gotten my license and took my parents' car. I took my brother and sister to school that morning, and my mother gave me her paycheck to get cashed. I went to the bank to cash it, went to a friend's house trailer, and did drugs with him. We decided to go to Florida together and get with some girls."

When he came back, he continued 9th grade and started playing baseball and football but was soon back with the same bad crowd. During his 10th grade exams, he said he, "had my dad's old car again and some friends wanted to rob a place. I told them I would drop them off and pick them up, but the police caught me and sent me back to the Juvenile Reception and Evaluation Center. I was 16 years old and had a one-year probation."

Overall, I can see that Terry had a very dysfunctional family situation. He was also very low functioning and easily led into trouble by others. The fact that he got badly hooked on drugs at an early age didn't help, but the system also didn't help by giving him so many chances and not holding him accountable for his actions. Terry felt that, "if they had been harder on me and locked me up sooner, it may have helped."

I also noted that there was no mention of church or any kind of spiritual interaction in Terry's life. What if Terry had been matched with a faith-based mentor at an early age who could have helped him with his academics, shared Jesus with him, and helped him meet good friends? What if he could have had exciting adventures at a Christian Camp? Again, I reflect on Terry's opportunity to respond to Christ at my camp; it brings great sadness to my heart! I have thought about the question he asked me about running and wondered if I should have pursued the question more. Life is made of choices and as it has been said many times, "Show me your friends, and I will show you your future."

And so it was that on January 10th, 1986, Terry was given his last meal. He sat at a table with an empty chair beside him to represent a place for Jesus. He was taken to the electric chair and executed. He was 26 years old. I told Terry in a letter that I would come and pray with him if he desired, but I was not called. I was glad, as I didn't know how I would have handled it. In the end, I felt a deep sense of failure. I cried out to the Lord, "Lord, don't let me lose another one like this again!"

Chapter 7

Eric Waugh—God's Ambassador to Five Georgia Prisons

The day the phone rang at 10 a.m. in Atlanta, Georgia, was a cool, miserable spring day after an unusual snowstorm in the middle of April. I had wrecked my truck trying to make it to the condo where I lived in Decatur, Georgia, a few days earlier. The person on the other end of the line was Cheryl Penny, Eric Waugh's juvenile court counselor. As soon as I heard her voice, I knew something was terribly wrong.

When Eric was 16, he was sent to Lorenzo Benn Youth Development Center on November 19, 1990 because he and his brother Eric Prince had been arrested for murder. After serving two years at the juvenile center, Judge James had allowed us to place Eric in Ben Lippen instead of sending him to prison. In early August 1992 leading up to the school year, I had met with the admissions director at Ben Lippen to see if they would admit Eric as a dorm student.

It was one of the biggest miracles of my 35 or so years of ministry with troubled and institutionalized youth when Ben Lippen agreed to interview Eric and accepted him as a high school boarding student. I only had to pay his $35 application fee and promise them I would raise the $10,000 to cover his first year of school there. Added to this miracle, the Georgia Board of Pardons and Paroles voted on December 22nd to give Eric a very rare "Educational Reprieve" so he would not have to complete his seven-years to life sentence if he completed high school at Ben Lippen and stayed out of trouble. He would most likely be placed on adult probation and allowed to go on to college to prove himself for the rest of his sentence!

Unfortunately, the District Attorney of Douglasville, Georgia, who was strongly against this reprieve, notified Ben Lippen and placed an article in the local paper in Columbia, South Carolina, stating that they had accepted a convicted murderer at Ben Lippen who was a danger to the school and community. But although Ben Lippen was fully aware of Eric's charges, they knew he had a perfect record during his stay at Lorenzo Benn YDC. They also knew Eric's mom was dying of cancer and that Judge James thought Eric deserved a chance because of his youth at the time of the crime. They also knew it was his older brother, Eric Prince, who threw the fatal rock off the bridge that killed Mrs. Smail, a lady in a car on the interstate. All of these factors persuaded Ben Lippen to take Eric on.

Eric's two years at Lorenzo Benn YDC was a time of exceptional growth and accomplishments. He was a top academic student who never got a negative write-up and won every contest he entered. At only 5'6", he was an excellent athlete who could almost dunk a basketball. He played both basketball and football at Ben Lippen and received a most valuable player award in football. I was able to witness him run a punt back for a touchdown in the one game I attended.

But all this changed during Eric's spring break in April 1993. Although he had been strongly warned by his court counselor, Cheryl Penny, and I that the district attorney was out to get him, Eric agreed to go out in the middle of the night with friends who had alcohol, drugs, and a gun. The rest is history. Eric spent a total of 28 years in custody, including jail, juvenile, and adult corrections.

When I got the call, in a matter of seconds, I had to come to grips with the hard, cold fact that everything I and several others had worked on for many hours and many months was flushed down the drain. I don't remember a time when I was angrier at a young man I worked with. His mother was dying and instead of seeing him graduate from one of the best Christian boarding schools in the nation, she would die with him in prison. Everyone who knew him was devastated.

I know that all of us had worked on enough juvenile cases by this time that this should not have been a big surprise. Eric had not made a profession of Christian faith, and as we found out later, he was playing the game behind the backs of all of us while he was at Ben Lippen. The fact is that Eric is about the most intelligent young man I have ever worked with. He had great potential, and all of us could see that. We wanted to believe he was "over the hump," so to speak, as far as his addictions and manipulations were concerned, but he wasn't.

I think this has happened to me and others a number of times because we so much want to see a young man or woman reach the potential that we know they have, but we are strongly pushed to succeed, too. We want to have a "winner" and look back at all the work we have done and see our accomplishments. In addition, we want our financial supporters to feel that their investments in us and the high-risk kids and families are paying off.

However, in the end, we see that we can't shortcut the process. God must take each person, including each of us, through what each of us needs to go through for all of us to come to the end of our rope. He wants us to begin our dependence on Him and the power that only He can give us to make us overcomers by His grace and mercy.

Over time, Eric became a full believer in the finished work of Christ on his behalf. He led Bible studies in five different Georgia prisons and even earned a doctorate while he was spending his years in the prison system. I visited Eric four or five times over his 25 years in the adult system and even held a memorial service for his mom after her death in 1993. Eric was allowed to attend the memorial in an orange jumpsuit with handcuffs and restraints. It was a very difficult time for him and everyone there. I also attended Mrs. Waugh's funeral service.

That day I got the call telling me Eric was arrested was one of the saddest days of my life, very similar to the day Terry Roach was executed in Columbia in 1986. There was a deep sense of loss and failure, as if Satan won the day and robbed me of all the victories and successes that we had initially seen in Eric's case. In the end, God was going to win, but at the time, all I could see was failure and the power of our failed human nature and the sickness of our fallen flesh!

I always try to ask myself what factors involved in the life of a high-risk kid who has had a major fall. Eric wrote a book *From Dummy to Doctor* and said the following: "My dad became an alcoholic. My mom also drank, and they fought a lot. It was mostly verbal, but at times, it would get physical. I can remember my dad jerking my mom around by the hair of her head. At times…my dad would throw and bust glass jars full of vegetables we had picked out of our garden. One time, he chased my mom out the front door of our house at night with his 12-gauge shotgun and shot it into the air while my mom ran through the yard. My brothers and I were in the house and did not know that he had shot into the air. We thought he had shot her." Eric was between 7 and 10 years old when this happened.

However, it is important to note that Eric did not try to lay blame on his parents for his bad decisions and choices. He stated, "I accept full responsibility for my choices and my decisions. I do not blame my parents, circumstances, or anything else. However, there is not much doubt that raising a kid in that type of environment can have an extremely negative effect on that child's mental, emotional, social, and spiritual development." Eric goes on to share that he "began exhibiting destructive behavior at a very young age. Between the ages of five and nine, I was skipping school, getting into fights at the bus stop, and throwing eggs at the bus." Eric goes on to state that by the time he was fifteen years old, "I was an alcoholic. I would drink daily if I had the money and resources to get it."

This kind of dysfunctional family can be repeated many times over with the young men I have worked with over the years. One young man had a mom who had numerous live-in boyfriends. One of her boyfriends had some land in the country outside of Charlotte where the boyfriend and his mom would grow pot to use and sell. The young man began doing the same thing—using and selling pot to his high school friends.

Another thing that is common with high-risk youth is the instability of their home. There is a real pattern of moving from place to place and having to change schools a lot. They tend to get behind in school and lose all motivation to give any real emphasis on learning. Eric refers to this when he shares: "My mom struggled financially, and when I lived with her, we changed residences several times. Because of all of the moving, I had to change schools a number of times; therefore, I continued to have problems at school and to struggle academically because I did not apply myself."

Another principle that usually sticks out when working with high-risk youth is the fact that "birds of a feather flock together." Eric gravitated to his stepbrother, Eric Prince, who was several years older. Eric Waugh said they shared a bedroom and "smoked marijuana, drank alcohol, and partied on a regular basis." Eric states, "I started shoplifting, burglarizing homes and cars, vandalizing businesses, homes, and cars, etc."

As I reviewed my own childhood, I know there were certain times when I was very close to being drawn into some dangerous situations. One time when we had one of our rare snowstorms, I was with a group of neighborhood guys who decided to throw snowballs at passing cars on a main street of our area. At one point, some of the boys began putting rocks inside the snowballs. A car was hit, and the driver stopped to run after us; he was very close to getting the police involved. I've thought back at that time and wondered, "What if one of those snowballs broke the window of a car and caused a serious accident?" We were only thirteen years old at the time, but we could have gotten very serious charges. But for the grace of God, I could have gone in a very negative direction in my young life.

Statistics tell us the peer group is the most powerful influence over the lives of teens and youth through the college years. That is why it is so important that parents work hard at getting their children involved in positive peer groups. When I got my foster son, Matt, one of the first things I did was find him a positive peer group in the neighborhood that loved playing basketball. My foster son loved and lived for basketball continually. This group of four guys were all professing Christians and were a positive influence on Matt; without them, I don't think Matt would have made it through high school. Thanks to God, this group, and other mentors, Matt became the only member of his family to graduate from high school!

As I mentioned above, Eric came out on top in the end. He was allowed to be the Lord's missionary to five different Georgia prisons where he led Bible studies and was involved in discipling a number of prisoners who turned to Christ while in prison. Eric came to accept that God had called him to do this, and he knew the Lord was going to have him released when the time was right.

He was far more patient than I was, but in 2019, he was finally released. Eric began to work hard at a meat company near Atlanta and was able to earn a week of paid vacation. His parole officer allowed him to go to a Christian conference in Florida during his vacation. My wife and I stopped by to see Eric and have breakfast with him on our way back to Iowa from Charlotte. That was one of the most joyful days of my life. I saw a very mature young man who was very motivated to be used by God wherever possible. He just turned 45, so he was really a young man anymore, yet he has many more years ahead of him where I believe God will use him to touch the lives of many.

I am very blessed to have known Eric and work with him, and I see him as a close brother in Christ. I value his friendship and all the experience he has had in ministering to incarcerated men throughout Georgia. My main prayer for Eric now is that he will find a supportive church and a godly woman who will be just the right ministry partner for him in the years ahead. To God be the glory, great things He has done!

Chapter 8

Working with Dysfunctional Families

The term "dysfunctional family" is thrown out quite a lot, but I am not sure a person can really understand what it is like until you spend some time staying with or doing several hour visits in one of these homes. Several years back, I visited a home where a single mom and her son were living. It was a pretty decent neighborhood in a university community. When I entered the apartment by way of the kitchen, I noticed right away that the kitchen was unkempt. There was a lot of bags of garbage that had not been taken out, dirty dishes in the sink, and very dirt floor. The rest of the house was in about the same condition. The mom was shifting most of the blame on her teenaged son. He had been coming to our YFC weekly clubs and going to our local campouts beside a good-sized lake where we fished.

One thing that I have noticed in just about every dysfunctional home I have ever gone into was just what I noticed in Travis's apartment: animals were abundant! There was a dog, a cat, a bird, and a large lizard. All of these had to be fed, yet the mom didn't have enough money to feed herself and her son. It was interesting to me that the pets seemed to be higher up on the priority list than the humans in the house. I have seen this over and over so many times that it has become almost expected when I am introduced to a new high-risk family.

Another family that I worked with had three dogs, a cat, and a large snake. The dogs were quite large, and they lived in this smaller trailer home with the three kids, a mom, dad, and often one or two guests who would be visiting from Chicago to deliver drugs. And even another family I worked with had a rabbit, a cat, a dog, and a horse!

I was baffled by this fact for quite a bit until I began discussing this with a friend of mine who had a good bit of experience with high-risk families. Finally, we came to the conclusion that these pets were the ones who gave them the much-needed unconditional love and acceptance. These pets didn't care what kind of clothes their owners wore or if they were using or dealing drugs, smoking several packs a day, or even if they had lice in their hair. As long as the animals were getting fed, they continued to show their owners love and acceptance with no conditions attached.

I began to realize more and more that the human need for acceptance and love causes people to go through all kinds of extreme hardships to get these needs met, even when it meant not meeting the basic needs of their children—food, clothing, shoes, etc. The drive for love and acceptance is very powerful and leads both youth and adults to look for love in all the wrong places, much of the time with tragic results. No one can effectively work with high-risk kids today without showing a very genuine caring heart that is consistent. At the same time, you must never make promises you cannot keep.

Sex for a large number of high-risk youths becomes a recreational sport. Because of this, many are bisexual, in that they have programmed their bodies to get a sexual high with both the same sex and the opposite sex on a regular basis. One young man told me his brother took him to a tree house when he was 10 or 12 years old and introduced him to oral sex. A short time later, this older brother brought a young girl up to the treehouse and taught him how to have intercourse with her.

Many troubled teens learn to sell their bodies to adults in order to secure food, transportation, a "safe" place to stay, among others. They learn how to feel out adults indirectly to see if they are open to having a sexual experience with them in such a way that if the adult is open to it, they can become more direct; if not, they can move toward just getting the adult to feel sorry for them and give them a meal or pay for a night in a motel, etc.

I encourage all those who are paid staff or volunteers who are working with high-risk kids to set boundaries both when it comes to physical touch as well as time commitments and commitments concerning what favors are done for them concerning money. You want to be a genuine caring person who helps them get the help they need when you can, but sometimes, there is a thin line between doing this and being used in the wrong way.

Years ago, a single mom with four children called me and told me her water was about to be turned off; she asked if I could help her pay this bill. She told me she had a good amount of money coming in from a lawsuit, and when that came in, she would pay me back. I told her that I could only do it this one time, and I was not giving to her out of any of my extra money; I was giving to her out of my need. I went and paid her water bill directly to the water company.

A few weeks later, a friend of this lady told me that she must have gotten her settlement with the hospital she had sued because she saw her "buying out Walmart." She was buying a tv set and lots of stuff, along with a used car. I figure she would soon be calling me to come and give me the $75 she owed for paying her water bill. I did get a call from her a week or so later. She called to ask if I could lend her some money to put gas in her car so she could get to the store and around town. I kindly reminded her what she owed me and turned down the opportunity to help her again. She never repaid me and never called me for money after that.

This was a lesson that I needed to learn about financial boundaries in working with high-risk families. The maturity that is so often lacking seems to lead them to practice using people as a way of life. So, as long as a person can find people to use, they never will learn to be responsible.

Having said this, I can say that it is never easy to strike the right balance. Sometimes, I allow myself to be used, as long as I am able to give direct help for kids that need food, shoes, and other basic needs when it is clear the parents are going to continue to invest in their own need for drugs, alcohol, and cigarettes instead of supplying the basic needs of their kids. I have served and purchased hundreds of meals for high-risk kids, and I have purchased quite a number of shoes and clothes so these youth could attend a Christian camp and be accepted by the other kids. I don't regret any of this. I just thank the Lord that He provided me the money when I needed it to help those I was called to serve. And I know many volunteers and other staff who have done the same thing as I have, and I thank the Lord for them and their dedication in showing God's love and caring in this way.

Chapter 9

The Green Train

Gene was one of the most intelligent and perceptive young men that I have worked with in 30 years of ministry to high-risk youth and families. He was sent to two different juvenile units in South Carolina in his early teen years. Gene's dad had him in his later life, at a time when he was quite addicted to alcohol.

On one occasion, Gene told me that he came back from his aunt's house with a bag of food that his aunt told him was only for him and his brother and sisters to eat, as she knew that Gene's dad was spending his money on alcohol. When Gene arrived home with the food and told his dad that his aunt wanted him to just share with his siblings, his dad, who had been drinking, got angry and grabbed the bag of food and threw it in the dumpster! After his dad fell asleep, Gene went out to the dumpster and got as much of the food as he could salvage and shared it with his family. Later, Gene's father had a faith experience, stopped drinking, and spent a lot of time reading his Bible and going to church.

One day when Gene was in a long-term juvenile unit in South Carolina, he asked me if I could take him on an off-campus trip on Father's Day so he could take his dad out to eat. He had saved up enough from his campus job to pay for all three of us to have a good fish dinner. I put in the request for the trip, and it was approved. I drove Gene back to his hometown area and helped him surprise his dad with a trip to a fish place. Gene's home was not too far from the beach, and there was a lot of good fish houses, as they were called where there was shrimp, flounder, etc. Gene's dad really appreciated getting to see his son and go out for this special meal.

I think over the years, alcohol had robbed Gene's dad of a lot of things and a lot of life experiences that many of us take for granted. On the way back to Columbia, Gene shared with me that he knew his dad had done a lot of wrong things to him and his family in his past life, but he said, "He's still my dad; I love him, and I want to show him respect." That was a day when I was extremely proud of one of the many young men I have worked with over the years. In my heart, I said, "Thank you, Lord, for letting me experience this moment in time."

Gene came to all our chapel programs and a lot of Bible studies, and he earned the right to go off-campus with me and several other kids on Wednesday nights to attend Cornerstone Presbyterian Church. They had a good meal and attended the high school youth group meeting there. This was always a special time of the week, which Gene and the others looked forward to having. One day when I was about 15 minutes late picking him up, Gene looked at me with a serious face and said, a bit tongue in cheek, "John, you are always late, but you never cancel." I took that as a compliment.

After he left the juvenile unit and returned home, Gene would call me every two or three months when he was about to get into trouble and go to jail. I would drive over to meet him and help him draw up a plan to get into a better situation. Occasionally, he would come and stay with me for a short time and then go home.

One time, he called me when he was living with a bunch of guys who were heavy drinkers. When I drove over and entered the house, Gene was the only one there, but there were beer cans everywhere. Gene came to live with me for a while and got a job at a grocery store. He was in a safe place for a while, and I felt good about that.

I finally pinned Gene down and said to him, "What do you really want to do with your life? You are a very intelligent guy and have a lot of potential, so what do you want to train for that can give you a good income?" Gene thought for a few moments and told me that he always wanted to be an EMT and a fireman. I was able to get Gene a scholarship for training in his hometown where he could live with his dad during training. What a joy it was for me to see Gene finally complete something positive for the first time in his life, it seemed.

One day when I was in the general area of Gene's home, after he had completed his EMT training, I stopped in to check on him. I first went to a restaurant to grab a bit to eat and a local paper. Of all things, there on the front page of the paper, in full color, was a picture of Gene putting out his first fire! He was holding the fire hose on a truck fire! I knew that had to be a God thing for me. The timing of that unplanned trip and the fact that I even purchased a local paper, which I hardly ever did, told me that God was in this, and I was so blessed to be a part of it.

Gene grew to adopt me as his second dad and would often call me on Father's Day to wish me the best and thank me for what I had done for him. Just the fact that he did this on a pretty regular basis told me about a part of his character that I didn't see in most of the youth I worked with. One quality that seems to be lacking today with so many is that of being a genuinely thankful person and expressing that appropriately and consistently.

I know my parents taught me to be thankful and my mother would remind me well into my adult life to be sure I thanked someone who did something for me. Gene had this side of him that showed a real concern for others and an ability to remain calm in times of stress and emergency.

I remember coming to his dorm one day when he was in a juvenile unit in South Carolina. He was about 17 years old at the time. When I saw him, his face was very swollen and black and blue all over, and his eyes were just half open. I asked him what happened, and he said very calmly that another student attacked him suddenly because he wouldn't give him any cigarettes. He told me several of his friends had offered to get locked up on purpose so they could go to the lock-up dorm and give that kid some "pay back." But Gene calmly stated that he told them not to do that. He said, "It isn't worth it."

Gene married a young lady that I was very impressed with and had a son that he very much adored. One day, he called me when I was living in Iowa and told me his wife had left him and gotten custody of his son. He was very upset and sounded a bit like he was considering suicide. I didn't think that Gene would do that, but I told him that if he needed to get away for a bit to sort things out, he could come and stay with me for a while.

Gene made the trip from South Carolina to Iowa the very next day. He began a job and started going to school to become a teacher. Gene was always good with writing and with English skills, so I encouraged him to train as a teacher. He didn't finish his training, but he got a job at a large junior high school in Iowa, where he worked for five or six years.

One day his girlfriend called me and told me Gene was getting the top award given to a teacher at his school after five years there. In the past, this award was never given to anyone unless they had been teaching ten or more years. Gene was so well liked by both teachers and students and did such an outstanding job as an assistant teacher working with the high-risk youth that they felt they had to give him this award. My wife and I attended the award ceremony and went out to eat with Gene and his girlfriend afterward. I must admit, that was another one of those proud "pa pa" days for me!

Gene went on to become a prison guard and was given primary custody of his son. He has done a great job raising is son in his upper teen years.

I have enclosed the story he wrote years ago when his wife had custody of his son and he had periodic visits with him. This was an award-winning story at the time, as he had this story selected for a community college publication. I will close with this story as it lets you know Gene's skill in writing, but it also reveals a lot about the negative side of divorce when children are involved.

I thank the Lord that I grew up in an age and time when people for the most part kept their marriage commitments and learned how to adjust through all the challenges and struggles that two trying to be one can bring. Thank you, Gene, for teaching me so much about what it means to grow up in a high-risk family and be an overcomer—not perfectly, but progressively, as we wait for God to finish His work in our lives until the day He calls us home.

When God did call Gene's dad home, he called me and told me that he took off work and went to be with his dad during the last days of his life. He told me that he held his dad and sang, "Jesus loves me" to him as he took his last breath. He told me, "I am not sure that I believe that, but I know my dad did, so I sang it for him." To that I say to Gene, "Yes, Jesus loves you and died for you and will not stop calling out to you until the day you die. His Spirit is the 'hound of heaven' and may He keep 'hounding' you until He brings you home."

The Green Train by Gene W.

It should have felt good to be back in such a familiar place, but this occasion was different. I was here to leave a part of me.

It was around one o'clock in the afternoon when I turned onto Anderson Field Road with my five-year-old son, Cole. I stayed on the wrong side of the road at first to avoid the rough bumps on the right. I knew it would smooth out just before the bridge that covered the small creek. It looked the same as ever. The sharp curve ahead still had the street sign knocked down from some careless driver not paying attention.

You see, I knew this road well. I had built a home here and started a family. I thought about the time my ex-wife and I brought Cole home from the hospital after he was born. That day I felt like I was the king of the world. I had made something that could never be taken away from me, or so I thought. I had brought him home to our castle to always protect and care for him. Yes, this road carried a lot more than cars; it was also a road of memories.

I had gone through a divorce two years earlier and moved to Iowa. Cole still lived with his mom in South Carolina.

The memory of our time together was all I had when he was gone. I would often think back to the day when he was born. Cole had been delivered by an emergency C-section. I was fortunate enough to have been there to watch it. He was blue at birth because he went into stress in the womb. After I knew he was okay, I had to laugh a little. It was as if I had become the proud parent of a Smurf. Then, when I heard his first cry, it felt like it wrapped around me and poured a newfound feeling inside me. It was a feeling of immense love that was overflowing and pouring back out of me by way of joyous tears.

Cole was breast fed, so I was unable to contribute to his feedings. I felt jealous during these times because I could not be the nurturing parent. His mother promised I could give him his first bottle. That was the day that I finally felt like his provider. Cradling him in my arms and watching him drink from the bottle, I came to understand the trust that a child has in his parents. He looked at me like he knew who I was and that I would always be there for him. I had made this a promise, but could that promise be fulfilled from 1,000 miles away?

Cole had come to spend the Christmas holidays with me, and although it had been a while since I had seen him, I could tell he was starting to become a little man. He was getting older, so he was starting to develop a real personality. I could tell he was becoming a little jokester. He would often come up behind me and shout, "Boo!" I always knew he was there but never let him know. I would jump up as if to be startled, and he would laugh until he was lying on the floor crying. He also had a side to him that wanted affection. He would enjoy sitting in my lap after dinner and watching a movie with me. He would look up at me from time to time just to say how much he loved me or missed me. I would say the same in return with a reassuring smile. It was perfect—just hanging out with my little buddy, like a father and son should. My heart always felt so whole at those moments.

It was time to take him back to his mom. I saw the house as I rounded the last corner. I knew this was not going to be easy. Who was I kidding? As if I could prepare myself for something like this. This was going to be beyond difficult. It was like the feeling you get when you watch a news story about someone who has abandoned their kids or done something to hurt them. That same gut-wrenching feeling (how could this happen to a kid?) was what I was dealing with now.

I turned into the driveway and slowly rolled to a stop, trying to prolong giving my son away as long as I could. I could hear the clicking of the seat belt in the back seat as Cole unbuckled himself. It had only been two years earlier that he had to ride in a car seat. I had to smile at the thought of how independent he was becoming.

As I walked Cole to the house, I wondered if he remembered when I would see him again. I had bought him a calendar before we left Iowa that had photographs of trains on it. I showed him the month of May, which had a picture of a big green train. I guess it looked like any other train I had seen, so I did not think much of it at the time. "Daddy will be back on this day to get you, son," I assured him, as I circled the 25th of May. He did not really seem interested in anything but that big green train. I was sure he could not grasp the idea of what a month was, much less five, but it felt good to just hear him say, "Ok, Daddy."

Now standing on the porch, I looked down at Cole. His hair blew in the wind and fell across his face. I pulled it back to see his face, much like pulling a curtain back to peek outside, only I was peeking in. The few freckles across his nose were light in color and looked like they had been sprinkled on with a peppershaker. His big blue eyes looked like glass with the sun reflecting off them. I was taking a picture with my mind, promising myself that I would remember just the way he looked when I left him, so when I got him again, it would be as if I had never left.

I knelt there to give him a hug and pulled him tightly into my arms, burying his face into my shoulder. I could feel his little fingers squeezing around both my shoulders, much like the way someone would squeeze a fruit to see if it were ripe. We were unaware of anything else around us. I held him so tightly it felt like we would mold into each other, becoming one. This hug of all hugs seemed to last forever, yet it ended much too soon.

My sadness began to engulf my whole body. It caused a physical pain in my chest. I knew this was my heart breaking. I could feel the tears in the corner of my eyes, just waiting for me to open the dam. They wanted—no needed—to run freely down my face, but I could not allow it, not yet. I had to be strong for him; besides, I still had 1,000 miles to go to get home. I had plenty of time to cry.

I could hear thoughts in my head that sounded so loud I was sure those near me could hear them. *This is my son. This cannot be right. A son needs his father. Cole would not even be here if it had not been for me.* The thoughts were coming so fast I could not keep up with them.

Now was the time to say, "Goodbye." As I looked him straight in the eyes, I told him, "Cole, Daddy loves you and I will miss you, Buddy. I'll see you in May." His eyes looked into mine as if to say, *"No Daddy, stay here, please; I'll do whatever you want."* There was a moment of silence, and then he spoke. He did not blurt it out as you would hear from someone who is excited, but soft spoken, with a hint of a quiver. That quiver was my cue that my little five-year-old son was on his mother's porch trying to be strong for his dad. "Daddy," he said, "I'll be waiting for you." With this, I turned to leave.

Getting into the car, I could feel the dam in my eyes slowly being pulled back, causing my vision to blur. Wiping my eyes, I could see Cole running towards the car. I slung the door open with such force it slammed back into me. I jumped out of the car to give my boy one last hug. I knelt there with him in my arms wanting this to never end. Then Cole looked right into my eyes and said, "Daddy, I'll see you on the green train."

Chapter 10

I Dare You to Be a Part of the Answer!

I grew up in the generation where you could be dared and even double dared to do something thought to be extreme or a bit dangerous, but I was not one to be quick to take up a dare or to live dangerously. Looking back, I think the dare that I ended up taking really came from the Lord when He called me to move away from preparing to teach and coach in a private school or serve as a youth minister or a camp director.

Instead, He called me to take the challenge of working with high-risk kids and families and institutionalized youth.

A friend of mine, who was a schoolteacher by profession, once asked me a very pointed question when he said, "John, if you don't (work with high-risk kids), then who is going to take your place? I couldn't answer that question, and God seemed to use that question to help convince me to stick with it and not get out and go to a more comfortable place of service.

Yes, mentoring high-risk kids can be dangerous at times: I've had my life threatened at times. I've had a gun pointed to my head. I've been in the middle of several dangerous fights. That does, at times, come with the territory. But I also know the great joy that comes from seeing one of my kids graduate from high school. I've seen another join the Navy and invite me to attend his basic training graduation. I've been invited to take a tour of his ship. And another received a top award given to teachers and teacher assistants at a large junior high school near Cedar Rapids, Iowa.

Years back, my wife, Pat, and I were invited to attend the wedding of one of my students who had graduated from the State Training School in Eldora, Iowa. This young man grew tremendously in his personal faith and maturity while he was at the Training School and was able to go into the construction business, where he became a supervisor. He moved to a state west of Iowa with his wife and little girl to continue his construction work and be close to his mom. For several years, I got a Christmas card from him with a picture of his little girl!

To know you played an important role in the life of these young men and a good many more over 30 years is very rewarding! I have also learned from experience that nothing you seek to do for God's kingdom will ever be easy or uncontested by others. But I also know that, in the end, the rewards are awesome.

The present generation, much of the time, seems to be "all about me." A long-term commitment to anything is not common today. So, if you cannot commit to a long-term relationship with a troubled youth, this mentoring ministry is not for you.

I had two businessmen in the Coralville area of Iowa who took up the challenge to mentor several high-risk young men in the Iowa City area. About five years after I had left Iowa City, I got together with these businessmen and found out they had continued to work with their mentees after they had graduated from high school. They helped them get job training, secure a job, and even at times, bailed them out of jail to keep them moving in a positive direction! I was blown away when I heard how committed these men were in working long term with the two boys that they were matched with so many years before.

One of these mentees lost his mom, and his dad had been sent back to Mexico after breaking the law. He was without any family, but his mentor became his dad in many ways, and he even paid the way for this young man to go and visit his dad once a year for several years!

I know that mentoring high-risk boys and girls isn't for everyone, but I know that it is a ministry that far more readers need to be seriously considering. There are good opportunities with Youth for Christ, Young Life, and other government-run agencies that will train you and supervise you in getting set up with the right kid and family. This is a ministry of long-term success, not short-term. It also involves lots of disappointments and bad choices to work through. Yet, when you look at all of life, this is pretty true for all of us!

We all have had bad choices in our lives that we can learn from and share with others. Many of us have had our different forms of "prodigal son" experiences that have come close to destroying our lives and our futures. But in the end, we are stronger and wiser and are made overcomers by His grace and mercy.

God is using many "prison missionaries" for the rest of their lives, but it is bringing them joy and fulfillment to be used by God and to be able to send others out of prison to live changed and productive lives. I worked with a dedicated lady in her 50s who had an enormous impact on a 16-year-old young man in long-term juvenile corrections in South Carolina. She worked with him as a volunteer. She met with him twice a week to help him with his reading skills as well as his personal hygiene. When he left the juvenile unit in Columbia to return home to a small community near Clemson, South Carolina, he had raised his reading level three grades and greatly improved his communication skills and personal hygiene!

Jimmy, this young man, wrote me a letter about two months after he went home to ask me if he could talk with the church that I had taken him to on several occasions. He wanted to see if he could go with them on their summer trip to Mexico. He said that he felt like God wanted him to go. I contacted this Presbyterian church, and their leaders asked me to bring Jimmy to talk with them. I made the trip up past Clemson to his little community. I found a small, broken-down trailer in the middle of a corn field.

Jimmy got into the car and rode back with me to Columbia for a day trip the following Sunday. He met with several leaders of the church who interviewed him and asked him questions about his faith and his desire to go with them on this mission's trip to Mexico. The next day, after I had taken Jimmy home, a doctor from the church who had been part of the interview process called me and told me that he and the other leaders were very impressed with him. This doctor told me that he wanted to pay Jimmy's way to Mexico! He basically told me that whatever amount that Jimmy was not able to raise toward the trip, he would cover. Jimmy was very excited when I let him know that he had been approved and that a doctor was going to cover whatever he couldn't come up with financially.

The day came for me to pick Jimmy up at the McDonald's just across from Clemson University. I sat in my car waiting and hoping that his family would get Jimmy to me on time. After about 15 minutes went by, I saw an old, broken-down truck that reminded me of the Beverly Hillbillies. Something told me that Jimmy had arrived, and he had. He got out of the truck smiling as he pulled an ancient suitcase out of the back of the truck. The suitcase was tied together with two different pieces of rope. I greeted his dad and told him what time we would be back after the trip. His dad signed the parent permission form I brought from the church, and we took off for Columbia after grabbing a bite of lunch at McDonald's.

The group was gathering at the church that afternoon to spend some time in training and orientation before sleeping in the basement

of the church. Early the next day, the Mexico team left to fly to Me·
and begin a long week of ministry in cooperation with a Mexic.
church. I prayed hard all that week and asked others to pray for Jimm)
and this entire mission's trip.

When the group returned, I met up with them and got Jimmy back
to his home. As I recall, Jimmy was quite tired and wasn't able to tell me
much about the trip. I think he slept most of the way home.

Later, I talked with the doctor who had sponsored Jimmy for the
trip. He told me that Jimmy didn't do that well on the construction
project, but he did a great job getting kids to the evening rally meetings.
He told me that Jimmy was like the pied piper leading a big group
of community kids to the programs each night! This was important
because it was at the evening meetings that the gospel message was
shared with all who attended.

I was thrilled to hear that the Lord had used Jimmy in a very
specific way. I was also thrilled to hear that several months later, Jimmy
went to a community meeting a short way from Clemson. He told the
leaders at this meeting that kids were getting into trouble there because
they didn't have a positive place to go where they could play games and
have recreation. The community members were impressed with Jimmy's
presentation and ended up voting to raise the funds to build a youth
center!

To see the Lord take this kid from where he was when he first came
to the juvenile unit in Columbia to what he grew into after interacting
with a dedicated volunteer, attending Wednesday night youth group at
Cornerstone Presbyterian Church, and then going on a mission's trip to
Mexico, taught me never to sell a troubled kid short! When these kids
seek to follow a new life in Christ, it's not about their IQ. It's not about
their financial status. It's about a heart commitment that God looks on
and honors.

I like to think about Jimmy and a number of others like him when
I remember a conversation I had years ago with a new pastor of a small
support church that I visited to give a yearly report to the congregation.
This pastor followed me out of the door after I had given my presentation

the members I was talking with. He quickly told me ⌐ the church would not continue my $25 per month ⌐nt on to tell me that it was his personal feeling that the ⌐ I was working with was a waste of time. These kids, he felt, ⌐er change, but he thanked me for my efforts.

I wrote a final thank you letter to the church letting them know how much I appreciated the past support and prayers they had been giving me for several years. Soon after the sad encounter with the pastor, I received a letter from another church that I had applied to for support. They let me know they had voted to give me $100 per month. I just had to chuckle a bit about how God is so faithful to take what seems to be a loss at times and multiply it into a gain as only He can do!

I know that God wants to make mission impossible possible through you whether you work with high-risk kids or some other outreach or short-term ministry. Stuart Briscoe shared years ago about the four stages of the Christian life. I would like to briefly share these with you as I close out this chapter.

The First Stage: "This is easy"

This is when a person first believes the gospel. John 3:16 states, "For God so loved the world that He gave His only Son, that whoever believes in Him shall not perish, but have everlasting life." So, all we have to do is accept Jesus and what He did on the cross for us? This is easy. No problem!

The Second Stage: "This is difficult"

This comes as a person grows in their faith and comes to realize all that the Lord has called us to in Christ. Matthew 28:19 states, "Go therefore and make disciples of all nations, baptizing them in the name of the Father and of the Son and of the Holy Spirit." This sounds great, but how on earth are we going to do this? There are culture barriers, language barriers, transportation barriers, food barriers, and financial barriers! This is very difficult!

The Third Stage: "This is impossible"

Now we are faced with obeying some direct commands that seem impossible. Matthew 5:44: "Love your enemies and pray for those who persecute you." There is no way we can do this! Loving and praying for those who are persecuting us? God is now asking us to do the impossible, and we just can't humanly do this, can we?

The Fourth Stage: "This is exciting"

This is where we come to realize that we can't, but He can. The power that raised Jesus from the dead is available to enable us to do mission impossible! Paul tells us in Philippians 4:13, "I can do all things through Christ, who strengthens me." Yes, His job is to make mission impossible possible, and seeing Him answer prayers and work miracles through us makes the Christian life exciting. Seeing Him transform a person who has been a prisoner to alcohol all his life and see Him free that person and deliver him totally, never to return to alcohol for the rest of his life—that is exciting!

I don't know what stage you are in at this time in your journey with Christ, but it is my deep prayer that more and more you will be able to experience the stage of "This is exciting" as you see the Lord make mission impossible, possible over and over again!

I dare you!

Chapter 11

Memories That Last

Basketball Memories

Although I loved football deeply and enjoyed playing pick-up football on many occasions, I grew fascinated with basketball—especially coaching it. I sort of learned as I went along, but I knew that the high-risk kids I was working with were very much into basketball more than any other sport.

I made use of basketball with the high-risk boys and court referrals that I worked with for many years and in many ways. We formed teams and joined basketball leagues so that we could incorporate this with our weekly club meetings. We would practice basketball and then have a small group meeting discussing issues using principles from the Bible.

Two games stand out in my mind where I was coaching two different teams. The first game was when I was coaching a team made up of boys at Stonewall Jackson Training School in Concord, North Carolina. A friend that I grew up with was the youth director of an inner city church that had a gym. He put together a team, and we came to his church gym to play a game.

This team had a sharpshooter who was hitting from the outside. It was like he couldn't miss. Since I was playing a zone defense, he wasn't being guarded that well. They were beating us by ten points at half time and were very confident that they were going to win. They also implied that my guys were "making eyes" at their girlfriends in the audience—so they had even more motivation to beat us badly.

At half time, I decided to try a new defense. I put in a "box and one" defense with my best defender playing their sharpshooter man to man, while the rest of my team played an active zone defense. Their shooter did not make another basket for the rest of the game, and we won the game by ten points! I was a great comeback victory for us in a very difficult situation.

However, the inner city team we were playing got very angry at the end of the game and verbally threatened our players as we rushed them out to our bus to leave as quickly as possible. We rushed into the bus and took off. Two or three of their players got into a car, took the backroads, and got ahead of us. They got out of their car with a brick, which they threw at our bus as we passed them, knocking out a headlight out of the bus. Our driver turned around and headed back to the church to call the incident in and tell the youth pastor what happened. It was glad to see the inner city team had left and were gone from the church.

I really felt bad for my friend who went out of his way to set up this game, and I know he had no idea his team would act so poorly when they lost. But overall, it certainly made this a most memorable win for me. I was so proud of my players and the way they played their hearts out and responded to adversity to bring home the big come-from-behind win!

At another time, I was coaching a team from the community in Raleigh. It was made up of high-risk kids and court referrals from the community. I was able to get a game set up with the maximum-security juvenile unit, C. A. Dillon in Butner, North Carolina. We played at the gym located at C. A. Dillon. They loved having us come because they had very few teams willing to come in and play them at this secure unit.

My team played a close game, but we were one point behind with about 30 seconds left in the game. The C. A. Dillon team began celebrating and playing music on a tape player they had with them at their bench. But we had 20 seconds left to play, so I had my team bring the ball to half-court, where we called a timeout. There was about 10 or 12 seconds left to try to get a shot off. I told my players to push the ball inside and try to get an inside shot off or draw a foul.

My guys did take it inside, but then kicked it back outside on the wing and put a long shot up from there. Amazingly, the ball went in with 5 seconds left, and we were up by one point. The C. A. Dillon team brought the ball to just past half-court and tossed up a prayer. It failed to go into the basket, and we won the game!

I knew that again I was going to need to get my players out of there as quickly as possible. The C. A. Dillon team didn't like to lose, and we had stunned them pretty bad. So, I was glad they had a high security situation to control their players, which allowed us to get out of the gym and on our way to our van. It was another great comeback win for me as a coach, and I was again very proud of the effort by my players in yet another sticky situation.

I was also very thankful to the Lord for allowing us to be able to show these youth they were cared about in their need to have someone willing to come in and play ball with them. I know it caused them as well to have a growing respect for Chap. Sellers who could, as a Christian, bring a team in and coach the win!

Another basketball event I would like to share was when I was in Charlotte around 1995. I was helping with a Youth for Christ program there while I was waiting to find a full-time assignment to join in another town. A pastor friend of mine was an inner city pastor in Charlotte and was one of the official chaplains of the Charlotte Hornets pro-basketball team.

One day, he called me out of the blue and asked me if I would like to be a guest chaplain at the Charlotte Hornets game that night. I asked him if the Pope was Catholic and told him just to let me know when to meet him. After we met up, I attended the game through the VIP entrance. I gave a short devotional to the team, coaches, trainers, and any members that wished to attend. I also gave a prayer for the team. In addition, I was taken to a special seat just above the tunnel where the Hornets came into the arena to play. That night, the Hornets scored more points than they had scored all season and won the game! I told my friend they needed to ask me to be chaplain of the night more often!

Yet one last basketball experience has to do with the time I took a lady I was getting to know from Wycliffe Bible Translators to a North Carolina basketball game in Chapel Hill. She was an alumnus from the school and was looking forward to going to the game with me. We went out to eat and on to the game.

North Carolina was playing Wake Forest, who had a famous player named Duncan. Wake Forest was hitting about every basket they threw up, and Duncan was killing the Tar Hills. At the half, Wake was leading the Tar Hills by 35 points. I was desperate to see the North Carolina team come back so that they could at least make a game of it and lose by no more than 10 points or so. I felt that my date was not going to be happy seeing her old school get beaten and run off their own court!

Amazingly, Coach Dean Smith of North Carolina made some great half-time adjustments. His team played much better defense in the second half and came back little by little and finally tied the game up to send it into overtime. In the end, they won the game in overtime with one of the best comebacks in the history of college basketball. Needless to say, we had a very joyful ride home that night!

Football Memories

Football has played a big part in my life and growth for many years. The good Lord gave me a body for soccer or maybe lightweight wrestling, but I have always had a growing desire to play football and be a part of college football.

As a kid, my parents would not let me play football with the neighborhood boys, but when I was about 16 or 17, I was able to convince my mother that playing football with the neighborhood boys would allow me to build a relationship with them and help me model my faith. Since I could still go to church Sunday morning and evening, my mom allowed me to start playing football with the local boys on Sunday afternoons during the fall.

I learned how to rush the quarterback and make it difficult for him to throw a long pass. I also became good at running back kick-offs and got better and better at playing quarterback as time went on. I started practicing kicking the football over the tall bushes behind my house using my bare foot with no shoes on. I wanted to go out for extra point kicker in high school, but I didn't have the confidence to do it.

I attended just about every high school game that my high school varsity team played at their home field and a few away games as well. There are three high school games that stick out in my mind as I think back on my senior high years. The first was the first game of my senior year.

During the summer leading up to this fall season, our star quarterback, Jim Nash, lost his mother, his loyal fan for so many years, to cancer. His first game of his senior year at Memorial Stadium, Charlotte, would be the first time he played organized football without his mom in the stands pulling for him. He wanted to play the best game of his life. It was a very emotional time for him, and the pressure became too much. Instead of the best game of his life, Jimmy played what turned out to be the worst game of his life. He and the other Wildcats lost to Lexington High 48 to 0!

It was a very depressing loss, but I feel that Mrs. Nash was looking down on her son and saying, "Loss is part of life, Jimmy. Just keep on playing; better days will come." And better days did come, as Jim got six wins before the end of the season to go 6 and 4, overall. His big win came over North Mecklenburg. I think this was the game when he was really playing for his mom.

The Wildcats were down by 5 points with 41 seconds to play when they began a final drive at their 20-yard line. The first play, Jim was caught for a 10-yard loss. But from then on, he slowly worked his team down the field. With 8 seconds left on the clock, and the ball at the 29-yard line, Nash scrambled to his right, trying to get the ball to his star halfback, but that whole side was covered by the North defense. So, Nash turned around and scrambled back to his left.

Nash was left-handed, so he was going to throw the ball with his left hand as he rolled left. At the same time as he threw the ball into the left side of the endzone, he was hit by a defensive player on his right side and was down on the field. However, while he was down, the ball went into the hands of his receiver, Russell Meers, for the winning touchdown.

This was the greatest comeback that I ever saw in high school football, and to see it in person was very special for me. I think it was also very special for Mrs. Nash as she looked down from that cloud of witnesses in heaven. Jim Nash went on to play defense for the South Carolina Gamecocks, become a dedicated believer, and lead Christian businessmen in Columbia, South Carolina, for many years. Leaders learn how to be overcomers and don't let losses destroy their future. We can learn a lot from football!

My brother Joe began taking me to North Carolina football games when I was in my mid-twenties. These were very special days for me. We would leave early to drive from Charlotte to Chapel Hill. It was a time to visit and get caught up with each other as we drove. We had lunch at a special place in Chapel Hill and went to the game. On the way back home, we would stop at a barbeque place about halfway back. Usually, we were celebrating a victory. Occasionally, we were trying to overcome the disappointment of a loss.

These were very special times with my brother, and I will never forget them. When I can, I go back to a football game in Chapel Hill in memory of him, and all the past trips with Joe flow back into my memory. One of the most memorable games at Chapel Hill with Joe was when we attended a Carolina vs. Clemson game.

Carolina had lost to Clemson year after year for about 5 years in a row, often by about 3 to 5 points. But this year, the Carolina team threw a pass to the sideline just about 5 yards from the goal line and right in front of where we were sitting. There was little time left in the game, so after punching the ball in for the winning touchdown, the Hills were able to hold on for a big win! We were ready to rejoice and celebrate and were very ready for barbeque. It was a special day, and I was so glad to have that time with my brother.

From football, I think you learn the lesson that Winston Churchill shared in his famous speech, when he stated, "Never, never, never, never, never give up!" There were so many times in my life when I wanted to just give in and give up. I would take a long walk late in the evening, and I would hear the Lord speaking to me: "I will bring you through this. Don't give up. I am able to carry you through." By faith, I hung in there and trusted the Lord to work things out. He always did, and I learned from the game of life.

I battled with a low self-image much of my life, but the Lord used football as one of the things to help me gain acceptance from others and improve my self-image. I played in two games that stand out to me.

The first was a time when I went out with one of the young men that I was working with to a church college and career outing, where they were playing touch football. My team struggled to move the ball, and they finally turned to me and said, "Let's see what the old man can do." I went in and saw one of my players get behind the defense and head into the end zone. I was not a long passer, but since he was the only player that I could see who was open, I set my feet, pulled back my arm, and threw the ball with all my strength just a short way in front of the receiver.

The ball came in below his knees, and he was able to catch it for a touchdown. I realized right after I threw the ball that I had pulled my arm out of my shoulder socket. It would be the last ball I would throw that day, but I helped my team win the game and gained the respect of folks 20 years younger than I! Sometimes there is a cost involved in trying to gain respect, and sometimes we have to check ourselves to make sure it doesn't go to prideful ego!

In 1987, I went on a trip with college students who were younger than me to Israel. I brought along a football, and when we had some free time after dinner one night, we went out to play some touch football. We were in a nice grassy field right beside the sea of Galilee. The younger players on my team were not able to make much progress because all they wanted was to throw the long ball for an immediate touchdown.

They finally turned to me, and as I heard before, they said, "Let's see what the old man can do." So, the "old man" became quarterback and led them to three touchdowns, winning the game. In some ways, I felt like I was reliving my childhood, but in other ways, maybe I was just living it for the first time. But it felt good to be respected and accepted by those around me after so many years of being rejected.

My last football memory goes back to my high school years. One Friday night, my mom came home from work around 6 p.m. My dad was not coming home until late that night, and my sister and two brothers were gone that night as well. I told my mother I was going to leave at 7 p.m. to head to the Friday night home football game at Memorial Stadium in Charlotte. My mother asked me to stay home that night because she didn't want to be alone. I told her that I could always take her to the game with me, but I knew she didn't want to go. "How do you know what I do and don't want to do?" she asked.

So, me and my mom had a date to the game that night. She hadn't been to a high school football game since she was in high school, but we had a good time watching the game. I got her some popcorn, and we sat together high up in the stands on the home team's side of the field. As I recall, we won the game. That made the "date" even better.

Looking back, I realize that game was one of the few things that I ever did alone with my mom during the three years of high school. Since she worked full-time plus overtime my whole junior high and high school, my mom couldn't get to very many things. I was so glad we had this special time together.

I was able over the years to take a number of the youth I worked with to both college and high school football games. It helped me build relationships and model Christ's love and caring. I took one man, Wess, to a North Carolina vs. Duke football game at Duke. We had to park a mile from the game but got there in time for the kick-off. We both were pulling for the Tar Heels, but Duke was outplaying the Heels that day, and with little time left, North Carolina was down by several points.

I pretty much gave up on my team, but Wess was emphatic when he told me the Heels are going to win! The Heels had to score a touchdown and the time was ticking down, so they threw a pass to the sidelines to run it out of bounds and stop the clock. It was man-to-man coverage, so the Tar Heel's receiver faked like he was going to run out of bounds, but he cut back inside and ran for the winning touchdown.

Wess rejoiced with me, but then looked at me with a very serious face and said with deep conviction, "John, you don't ever give up on your team!" I learned something from Wess that day, and I tried never again to give up on my team or any "team" that I was ever a part of from then on.

Who Is Tutoring Whom?

I was honored when one day in high school study hall one of the beauty queens who ended up becoming homecoming queen came over and asked me for help with a geometry question. I had worked the equation out, and it seemed accurate to me, so I shared that with her with a good bit of confidence. We went to geometry class, and the teacher worked the problem out for us on the board. Turns out, I had not worked out the problem correctly, and my answer was totally wrong. I did not get another visit from Eve, the beauty queen, ever again.

At yet another time, I was working on homework in the library at Garinger High. The star quarterback and star halfback from our football team came over to my table to see if I could help them prepare for an Algebra exam. Again, I tried to help them as much as I could. I took the exam with them. Both of them got a B+, and I got a C-! Who was tutoring whom?

That became the end of my seeking to help tutor anyone else. I did get a pretty good laugh out of it. It was a lesson in humility for me and allowed me to be more aware of what subjects I was gifted in and what subjects I was not—especially in terms of tutoring!

Why I'm Not a Cat Person

Although I did have a cat named Wiskers when I was a kid growing up in Charlotte, I grew more and more into a dog person the older I got. When I was a Youth for Christ intern in Greensboro, North Carolina, my roommate got a crazy Persian cat. The cat would run from you and was only loyal to his one master.

My roommate left for the weekend and made sure I knew not to let the cat run out the door. I came back from the store and left one of my grocery bags on a table just outside the apartment at the top of the stairs. I later undressed to take a shower and put a small shower towel around me and headed to the shower, but on the way to the shower, I realized I had left my shampoo in the grocery bag outside my door.

As I opened the door and stepped out to get the bag, I saw the black Persian cat about to prance out the door. I quickly slammed the door only to realize the door automatically locks when you shut it. So there I was, locked out of my apartment with my roommate not coming back for 48 hours! What was I going to do? It looked like I was going to have to sleep on the floor outside my apartment until my roommate returned.

I prayed and thought hard and finally remembered that the landlord had told us that if we ever got locked out, there was a ring of keys hanging on a nail in the basement. I carefully made my way down the stairs, out the main door, and around to the basement. After 30 minutes of searching, I found the ring of keys, made my way back up to my apartment, and found the key that worked for my door. By that time, I wanted to throw that cat out the door, but I was able to control myself.

On yet another weekend, my roommate was gone again, and I had a friend from my home church coming to visit. He came on Saturday morning, was spending the night, and was going to church with me the next morning. Alan, my friend, opened his suitcase and laid it at the end of his bed. The next morning, we woke up only to find that crazy Persian cat had urinated on Alan's clothes during the night. I had to work hard to come up with some clothes between my roommate's things and mine so Alan could have something to wear to church. I felt terrible, and again, I was ready to kill that cat!

It wasn't too long before the internship year was over, and I was able to move away from that apartment, away from that cat. I think I must have thrown a party when that day came.

The Awesome Weekend That Never Happened!

I grew up in Calvary Church, Charlotte, with Daryl Graham, the nephew of Billy Graham. Daryl was a bit accident prone. One Sunday, he came to church on crutches. When we asked him what happened, he laughed a bit and told us he was out hunting rabbits on Saturday and got too excited when a big rabbit ran out in front of him. As he grabbed for his pistol, the gun discharged and shot him in the leg through his holster. This was just one of several such accidents that happened to Daryl during his teen years at Calvary Church.

On yet another Sunday, Daryl came to church again on crutches. When I asked him what happened this time, he told me he was riding in a car with another boy from the church on Friday night. A car pulled up beside them at a stop light just before the light changed. Another teen in the car beside them had a handgun. This kid mistook Daryl for another boy he was out to get because the car Daryl was in was the same kind and color of the car the kid was after. He mistook him and shot through the door and hit Daryl in the leg! Only Daryl could get caught up in an accident like this! The shooter was caught and made to pay the cost of Daryl's leg repair along with other charges.

Daryl, another fellow in our youth group (Eddie), and I all ended up going to Columbia Bible College our freshman year in 1968. Daryl and Eddie met their wives at CBC their freshman year and left school to get married the following summer! Columbia Bible College was a strict school at that time and didn't allow its students to get engaged or married before their junior year.

Daryl was big on hunting on weekends. He would spend every weekend he could going to his Uncle Billy's in the mountains at Montreat, North Carolina. At Columbia Bible College, we were allowed to leave for two or three weekends a semester. Billy and Ruth Graham, Daryl's aunt and uncle, allowed him to bring one student with him each time he came for a weekend trip. Daryl was going to take me along one weekend near the end of the school year.

When the weekend came for the trip, I was approved to take the weekend off, but on Wednesday, I checked with Daryl who hadn't yet heard from Billy. On Thursday, I checked again, but he still hadn't confirmed the weekend with his Uncle Billy. He told me that if he didn't get a call from his uncle that evening, most likely, we would have to go another weekend.

On Friday after morning chapel, I checked with Daryl for the last time. He told me his Uncle Billy still hadn't confirmed his coming, so he most likely would go another weekend. Therefore, after classes were over, I took a ride home with another student in my church who was going to Charlotte for the weekend. An hour or so after I left for Charlotte, Billy Graham called Daryl to confirm that he could come to Montreat that weekend and bring a friend!

That ended up being the last weekend Daryl went to his uncle's house. And since he didn't return to college the next year because he got married, I never got the chance to spend a weekend with the most popular evangelist the world has ever known. It just became the awesome weekend that never happened.

The Big Sunday Surprise

Bill Harding was one of the first missionaries that Calvary Church in Charlotte, my home church, began supporting on a regular basis. He and his wife Elaine had five children, and they ministered in Ethiopia for many years. Bill and his family were headed back to Ethiopia for their second term there. The elders at Calvary asked him to speak on the Sunday morning before they were to head back to the field the following Wednesday. My dad, who was in the moving business, usually helped them pack what they were to take with them.

Bill arrived early and went into the little prayer room on the left side of the front of the auditorium to pray with the elders before the service started. Bill's mind was on his message as he entered the auditorium, so he was not paying attention to who was out in the audience. The service began with opening songs, announcements, and prayers. Finally, Bill was introduced as the missionary who was headed back to Ethiopia with his family.

Bill got up to give his message, a bit nervous as he wasn't too experienced yet in speaking to large crowds. As he looked out into the auditorium, there, halfway down the middle section of the pews, sat Billy Graham with his parents. Bill told me he became so rattled that he could hardly remember the key points of the message. He struggled through the rest the best he could and tried not to think about the fact he was preaching to Billy Graham!

After the final amen, Bill Harding went out to the foyer to greet the people and get their well wishes for his second term. It wasn't long before Billy Graham made his way to the foyer to greet Bill. When he arrived, Bill looked at him and said, "Oh, Dr. Graham, I shouldn't have been preaching to you today; you should have been preaching to me." Billy looked Bill Harding in the eyes with a serious expression and said very firmly, "Don't you ever say that! You are a missionary, and I'm not worthy to tie your shoes!" Bill told me later that he was so overwhelmed at Billy's response that he almost melted into the floor!

This was my best memory of Billy Graham, the one we called "Uncle Billy" growing up in Calvary Church where Billy's mother, dad, sister, and brother attended. I felt very blessed to know this family and be influenced by them over my early years. Mother Graham, Billy's mom, was known as a very dedicated prayer warrior. She would call people to get prayer requests and have people call her. She spent many hours in prayer for many people.

At Christmas, the youth of the church would always go Christmas caroling, and we would always stop by Mother Graham's house. She would be waiting for us with hot chocolate and homemade cookies. It was our favorite place to go caroling, and it was the last stop on our tour.

The Night They Pulled the Plug on Jesus

I had the privilege of working with Camfel Productions out of California once a year for 25 years. Camfel has been the top multi-media school assembly program in the US for many years. This faith-based media company originally came out of Campus Crusade for Christ. They travel around the country during the school months with teams of two techs who are usually in their early to mid-twenties. Camfel travels with about two programs for junior high and senior high youth and two programs for grammar school youth. They also travel with a gospel version of these programs that can be shown at church youth groups and Christian schools.

A new program that runs about 40 minutes is produced each summer. Camfel uses feedback from teachers and principals to learn what issues need to be addressed, such as teen drinking, drugs, bullying and cyber-bullying, cutting, and the need to show respect for other students and those in authority. Camfel uses true life stories of youth who share what they have been through and how they were able to get delivered from these various issues that every youth tends to face during their school years.

In these 25 years, the Lord enabled us to present this production to a total of 20,000 youth and adults, including 1,000 grammar school youth. About half of his number were able to see the gospel version of this multi-media outreach.

I must say, for many years, my week spent booking and traveling with Camfel techs to many schools, churches, and juvenile institutions was the highlight of my year. My wife Pat and I always looked forward to hosting these Camfel techs in our home whenever possible. It was such a joy to work with these techs and seek to minister to them as they worked so many long hours giving one presentation after another—sometimes three or four in one day!

In the mid-eighties, I talked with the youth minister at my home church, Calvary Church in Charlotte, about showing the gospel version of Camfel to the junior and senior high youth groups on a Sunday evening. We were going to show this wide screen production on screens 15 feet high and 45 feet wide in the gym. When Pastor Ross Rhoads heard this, he decided to talk to his friend in Chicago who ran Youth for Christ in that area. He heard that Chicago had used this production for their yearly fundraising banquet, and it was very well received by the adults and youth there. Pastor Rhoads wanted to show the production as a city-wide outreach to all of Charlotte!

I talked to Ross and told him that I was not sure that some of the music used in this production would be very well received by some of the people, but he said the adults need to see first-hand what their kids faced and what they were listening to. Therefore, we set up the screens in the main sanctuary for a Sunday evening presentation.

The house was packed with both youth and adults. The building held about 2,000 people, and I don't think there was a seat left. The production started out with President Ronald Reagan taking the oath of office and went into some very loud music that mostly non-Christian kids listened to. However, it took segments of music that asked questions with no real answers. The first two-thirds of the production was mostly secular, but the final third was the gospel answer to the problems presented in the first two-thirds.

I was sitting with Pastor Rhoads in the front row; he was to give the introduction and a wrap-up at the end with a gospel invitation. Everything was going well until the program started into the final third section of the production. Right as the gospel was about to be presented, the equipment shut down, and it seemed the techs were not able to get it started again.

Regardless, I sent Ross up to give an extended wrap-up with an invitation for anyone who wanted to give their lives to Christ and see Him change them from the inside out. 25 youth and adults came forward! I had attended this church all my life, and I had never seen that many people come forward at one time.

After the program was over, I went back to see the techs as the pastor and some of the elders were meeting with those who came forward. The two techs were very upset, so I asked them what was wrong. They told me one or two of the deacons objected to the production and the music and asked them to shut it down. When they didn't, one of the deacons pulled the main plug out of the wall and wouldn't let them put it back.

I couldn't believe it, but I realized why I had a reluctance to show it to the whole church. Nevertheless, the Lord worked in a most unusual way, so I had to thank Him all the more now that I knew what happened. As far as I know, the deacon was disciplined in some way, but I never heard and never really wanted to hear about it. I was just glad he did not badly damage the expensive equipment.

I was getting ready to leave the church that night when I heard one of the young techs crying on the phone as he tried to explain what had happened. "They pulled the plug on Jesus," he said several times. I felt so badly for him, but I realized that Jesus still got His "plug in," and 25 people were introduced to a new life in Christ! The Lord's gospel prevails even when our plans don't go the way we intend.

I Remember Grandfather Mountain

When I was a child in the cradle, my parents would take me along with my brother Joe and sister Kris up to the beautiful mountains of North Carolina near Boone. Our church, Calvary Church, had control of about 50 to 80 acres of land just down the road from Hound Ears Lodge and Hebron Colony. Hebron was a residential treatment facility for male alcoholics. It was started by the first Pastor of Calvary Church. He moved to the mountains after leaving the church and began two facilities about one mile apart—Hebron County for the men and Grace Home for women.

The church camp was about 10 to 15 miles from Grandfather Mountain. When I was young, my older brother and others in the church talked about climbing over Grandfather Mountain. It became an annual event for many of them each summer during camp.

Grandfather Mountain got its name because as you drive up Highway 105 toward the mountain, you can see the five peaks of the mountain off to the left side of the road. These peaks, when viewed from a distance have the strong resemblance of an old man's face as he lies on his back with a nose, mouth, and chin.

I couldn't wait until I was old enough to climb Grandfather. I think I climbed it first when I was in the seventh grade. The hike took almost three hours to make it all the way over from the starting point on Highway 105 to the mile-high swinging bridge on the other end of the mountain. We had to park a van at the bridge end of the mountain then ride that back down the other side. Occasionally, we would hike all the way over and back again.

If you take the trail that goes over the ridge and five peaks, you must go over a number of cliffs using ladders made of ropes and tree limbs. If you fell off, you would fall quite a distance, likely to your death! My friend from church, John M., was climbing with a group of us guys one day. He was standing on a ledge looking out over a beautiful valley below when he slipped and fell. We were not looking in his direction when he fell, so when we looked back, John was gone.

When we went over to see where John had gone, we found out that he slipped off and fell on his back onto another ledge that jutted out just below. He was so relaxed when he fell that he didn't get hurt, and he was able to join us and finish the rest of the trail! Obviously, he was ten times more careful the rest of the way. John was a strong believer, and I felt the Lord wanted all of us to learn how we could depend on Him to protect us as He did John on that frightening fall.

I can't say exactly how many times I climbed Grandfather or took other kids over it over the years. I would guess I climbed it at least fifteen times all together. Looking back at some of the danger involved in some of those high cliffs, I don't think I would take high-risk youth over that trail today. Back in those days, it seems we were not as careful or as risk conscious as we are today.

I ran a special scout program at the Samarkand Manor Training School near Eagle Springs, North Carolina. We would take a group of about 8 to 10 boys at a time through the three-month program. At the end of the three months, we would have a rewards banquet where the scouts would be given all the awards they earned. Then we would pick up another 8 to 10 boys and go again.

I did that program for three years. By my estimation, about 72 boys went through this special scout program. All of the sessions ended with a trip over Grandfather Mountain. If they made it successfully, we rewarded them with a badge.

On one trip over Grandfather Mountain with one of the scout groups, two boys went ahead of us leaders. They had been told not to go further than our eyesight, but in their excitement, they charged ahead and ended up taking the wrong trail. They went up the short side of the mountain and back down the other side instead of going over the long, high trail over the five peaks to the swinging bridge. Eventually, the state trail guide found them and brought them over to the mile-high bridge to meet us in the end. Needless to say, they did not get their Grandfather badges!

One day, I was taking a very small group of guys over Grandfather. It was a cloudy and foggy day. When we got to the top of the small peak, the fog was so thick you couldn't see your hand in front of your face! We decided it would be better to go straight back down and climb Grandfather another day.

On another trip, the day was nice and clear, with the sun shining and the sky a bright blue. We had made it to the first peak and began hiking over the ridge on a nice, wide, shady path. I heard some footsteps behind me, and the youngest boy ran up and jumped on my back and wrapped his arms around my neck. I heard him say, "I love you, Chap. I love you, thank you."

At that moment, I realized this young man had most likely never been to the mountains, and he most likely didn't have a relationship with his dad who would take him hiking or fishing. This young man had a deep impact on me because I knew he represented a lot of the boys I have worked with over the years who were "too cool" to hug me and tell me they loved me in moments of gratitude, yet he did.

I will never climb Grandfather again, but I look back with fond remembrance, including the time I was at the mile-high swinging bridge when the wind was blowing over 50 miles per hour. I could lean into the wind with the entire weight of my body, and the wind would hold me up! I remember the fall days when the leaves were at their best color and the sky was a clear, bright blue. You didn't want to go back down the mountain but stay as long as you could.

A Dead Stick Comes Alive

I grew up in a home my dad built on a left over "key lot" in a very nice neighborhood off of Country Club Drive in east Charlotte.

I liked doing yard work and my dad had me take care of the flowers, cut the yard and trim the bushes.

One day before leaving town on his business trip, he told me to find a stick and tie up the rose bush on the left side of the front yard.

I went to the vacant lot next to our house and found a straight stick about two feet long. I used it to tie up the rose bush that was falling over using cloth strips.

About ten days later, when I was working in the area, I looked down to see that the dead stick that was tied to the rose bush was beginning to send out sprouts in several places!

I asked my dad if I could try to plant it in the yard and see what it would do. He gave me permission and I carefully dug it up ;and planted it in the front yard on the left side.

That dead stick grew into a big maple tree! Every time I was back in that neighborhood I would go to see that tree towering up beside the other pine trees there.

I have used this as an illustration of what God wants to do in our lives. He wants to take "sticks" that are totally dead in sin and make us alive in Christ and able to grow and mature into something amazing.

On my last trip to the old neighborhood I was saddened to see that the tree had been cut down. So, the life cycle has ended for this amazing tree. I thank God that he allowed me to experience such a wonderful example in nature of what He seeks to do in all of our lives! To God be the glory.

The Lord has given us so many awesome ways to enjoy His creation in nature. The Bible makes it clear that God has revealed Himself in nature. We can see His great creativity, along with His eternity, as we see the ocean waves rolling in over and over again. To God be the glory!

My memories after seventy plus years of life could go on for many more pages, but I will end here. Looking back, I know that there were many sad times and many challenges, but overall, I have had so many wonderful friends and experiences. My joy comes from knowing that I have a Lord who never leaves me nor forsakes me, and He enables me to continue to be an overcomer by His mercy and grace. To God be the glory!

Poems and Songs
by J. Edward Sellers

The following poems and songs are one I have written at different times in my life. They show different periods of growth in my life and times when I felt inspired by the Holy Spirit to put thoughts to paper.

Love of God (sung to the tune "Edelweiss")
Love of God, love divine, manifested in Jesus
Came to Earth, lived to die, joy and freedom to give us
Son of God and Son of man, sinner now believe Him
Love of God, rich and free, free to all who'll receive Him

A Great Man

A great man is just a shadow
God shines through the night
When a great man increases his greatness
He first increases the light!

If You Deny My Jesus (Song)

If you deny my Jesus, then look to the heart where He lives
If you deny my Jesus, explain the peace He gives
If you deny my Jesus and say He's not the way
Then show me another, who can turn the night to day.

If you deny my Jesus, and if He is dead as you say
Then tell me why I'm filled with hope by following Him each day?

He Made It Possible

He made it possible by dying on the tree
He made it possible by redeeming you and me
He made it possible cause His love is full and free
Oh yes, our Lord made life possible for you and me.

He made it possible, and He's a friend to stay
He made it possible, and I know He'll lead the way
He made it possible, so I'll live for Him each day
Oh yes, He made it possible, and He's coming back some day.

A Flaming Torch

Am I to be a flaming torch, a symbol holy, pure?
Must I all the sin and shame of this vile world endure?
Am I to reach great heights with God, while shunned by mortal man?
Must I live through brutal times, the prize of God to win?
If so, I will not shrink from this, but by God's strength I will endure.
For it is He who gives me hope and keeps me burning pure!

An Eternal Thing Each Day

Father, may I do an eternal thing today
　　In thought, in deed, or in what I say
Yes, help me do an eternal thing this day
　　That others might find the Christ-like way
And may it be said, when from this earth I pass away
　　That I have done an eternal thing each day!

Three Score and Ten

Three score and ten years are given,
　　Three score and ten to a man.
The paths to be traveled are many,
　　Countless are the opportunities at hand.

The decisions to be made are great ones,
    For they reveal to all your stand.
Thus, it will pay to base them on wisdom,
    Rather than selfish foundations of sand.

Three score and ten years are given,
    Three score and ten to a man.
But far greater than three score and ten years
    Are those spend in the Almighty's land!

Our Earthly Gardens

We're all planting a garden, as our earthly years go by
    But some of us act as if we know not why.
A few people plant with care, and so their gardens grow,
    They take out what's not needed and lasting things they grow.
But others take no care, the weeds they just let go,
    They bother not with lasting things; their gardens do not grow.
Yes, we are all planting a garden, it will be here when we die,
    For you see, my fellow planter, that's the real reason why!

Johnny Lee

There's some kids that major in English
There's others that major in Math
There's a few that major in chemistry,
But not Johnny Lee, he sets his sights on popularity.

Well Johnny he squeezed through with a mighty low grade,
    But you'd have to do a bit of talking to name the friends he
    made.
His senior year, he was riding high, and things were going great
    'til that day came when Johnny found himself about to graduate.

It was thus that round the wheel of life started poor old Johnny
Lee,
    With only lovely memories of what he used to be.

But Jesus, I'll Go (A lead into the song, "I'll Go Where You Want Me to Go")

But Jesus, nobody else is going
But Jesus, nobody cares
But Jesus, the cares of this world are calling
Yes Jesus, I'll go

But Jesus, I can't understand your calling
But Jesus, what will they say?
But Jesus, the way is long and narrow
Yes Jesus, I'll go

I'll go where you want me to go, dear Lord....

The Ideal Friend

The ideal friend is one with whom you can communicate thoughts, ideas, and troubles.

He is willing to listen to your point of view, and to give you his honest advice.

He gives freely of himself, without the thought of receiving in return.

A friend stands beside you when all others have given you up.

He is one who takes and shares your happiness as well as your sorrow.

But most important of all, he is one in whom you can put complete trust, without reserve, receiving his equal trust in return.

Appendix B

Lessons from Living Life in a Fallen World

What I have learned and am continuing to learn from living 70 years in a fallen world with fallen people like myself:

1. No other person has a right to put a value on my life or my person, but God only as He made me. So, I should not give anyone more power over me than what they deserve. I get my worth, my calling, my confidence, and my direction from a personal walk with my Lord.

2. Rejection is a big part of character building. How we respond to rejection is most important. Fallen humans tend to give criticism and "put downs" rather than encouragement and positive comments.

3. Denial always tends to be our first reaction to any bad decision or choice that we make. Owning up to our bad and sinful choices is the first step in learning from these choices and building Christ-like character long term.

4. Too many Christian leaders tend to move toward insecurity rather than a secure confidence in God as they gain more power over others.

5. If leaders are not careful, they will move toward using and manipulating others rather than developing others and helping them develop their full potential. This can also reveal a leader's insecurity.

6. One of the most important lessons that Christian workers and leaders must learn or be taught is the importance of setting and maintaining proper boundaries in working and relating to others.

7. God expects the local body of believers to not only share the gospel and exercise church discipline, when needed, but also to give a proper emphasis on restoring believers when they fall and are truly repentant. Every local church needs to work through this in advance and have a good Biblical plan available when needed. We need to celebrate recovery far more than "glorifying a fall." Nobody wins when we shoot our wounded!

8. Labeling others can be both harmful and destructive and make it much more difficult for the one being labeled to reach his/her potential. Self-centered, prideful, and cocky people are much more likely to be engaged in labeling.

9. Jumping to conclusions before you have all the facts can make a fool out of you pretty fast. Doing this puts one in a bad place of having to force the facts to prove your conclusions when they really don't. Pride can keep one from doing the right thing— just admit you were wrong and apologize.

10. Apologizing when you make a bad choice and when you are wrong enables you to grow and learn from mistakes and builds proper humility into one's character.

11. It's always easier to rely on medication than doing the hard work of finding the cause of a problem and helping a person work through that cause. It's harder to apply the power and promises of God to overcome issues and lay them at the foot of the cross and move on. Jesus died to deliver us from our sin and the sins of others committed against us!

12. If keeping with the Joneses becomes your goal in life, you will never be satisfied or fulfilled, and money can easily become your god. The key is to adopt the principle that Paul presents in Philippians 4:11-13: "I have learned in whatever situation I am in to be content. I have learned the secret of facing plenty and hunger, abundance and being in need. I can do all things through Him who strengthens me." (God provides for me and enables me to be an overcomer by His grace and mercy.) With this, life becomes peaceful and exciting.

13. The only thing in this life that really stays the same is God and His Word and His promises. Everything else in life changes and often, even disappears! We have the privilege of enjoying the good people and good things God has given us in this life while they last. We are not called to put our faith in terminal things. Building on God's calling and His eternal purposes lead to true peace and satisfaction.

A Special Word from the Author

You may be reading this book without a real assurance of a personal relationship with the Lord Jesus. The older I get, the more I have come to realize how short this life is; it's just a drop in the bucket in terms of eternity! The Bible teaches that the Lord has created us with a point or time of beginning and a soul that lives on forever after we leave our earthly suits behind. The Bible also teaches us that God created us for two main purposes: "to know Him and to make Him known." In the end, there is no greater joy that any person can have in this life than to know Jesus personally and to know His life-changing power of forgiveness, joy, and peace in the midst of this fallen world.

Following Jesus is not presented in His Word as a human works endeavor—it is presented as a work of God's Grace, a gift to all who will humble themselves and call on Jesus. Romans 10:13 states it very simply, "Whosoever will call on the name of the Lord will be saved."

John 3:16 is equally simple: "For God so loved the world that He gave His only Son, that whosoever believes in Him should not perish, but have eternal life."

If you have never done so, I challenge you to call on Him today, ask for His forgiveness and give Him control of your life. You will never regret it! Then, get involved in a good Bible-centered local church where you can grow in your faith.

As you move forward in what time you have left on this earth, I pray that you will seriously consider mentoring a high-risk boy or girl in your community as the Lord leads.

May you know His blessing and His power and the joy of following Him for the rest of your life! If you would like additional information call the Billy Graham Association, 888.388.2683.

Rejoicing in Him,
J. Edward Sellers
"Chap." John

Author Bio

Chaplain J. Edward Sellers was born in Charlotte, North Carolina, in 1949. He graduated from Garinger High with honors. In 1972, Chap. Sellers got his Bachelor of Arts in Bible with a minor in Education from Columbia Bible College (Columbia International University), where he served as a student association vice president and as a yearbook editor. In 1987, he received a Master of Divinity Degree with a major in Cross-Cultural Ministry and a minor in Counseling from Columbia International University.

Chaplain Sellers has served with Youth for Christ for over 25 years, working with high-risk kids and families and with long-term juvenile units in North Carolina, South Carolina, Georgia, and Iowa, with an emphasis in chaplaincy services.

During his ministry, he was known for trying new things, like fishing tournaments, all-night basketball tournaments (Midnight Madness), off-campus day camps, and overnight weekend camps, and he set up one of the first experimental juvenile halfway houses in the country for juvenile males coming out of long-term training schools in North and South Carolina. This program was built around apprentice jobs with faith-based employers.

Working with the recreation departments of state training schools in North and South Carolina, Chap. Sellers began a yearly all-star basketball game followed by an awards banquet that included an adult Christian athlete sharing his testimony. This yearly game ran for over 20 years straight without a break and was sponsored by Kiwanis.

Chap. Sellers identifies with the following quote by Robert Kennedy: "Some people see things as they are and ask, why? I dream things that never were and ask, why not?"

Chaplain Sellers states, "Everything that the Lord has enabled me to do has been mission impossible, but it has all been made possible by the grace and mercy of God. To Him be the glory, great things He has done!"

Would you like to contact the author? You can email him at, sweetchili401@gmail.com

Financial Sponsors

As this book goes to print, the following people have given financial gifts to make this publication possible. A deep appreciation to each of them!

Ed and Jacki Bateman
Alan and Kathleen Baughman
Carol Best
Clark and Barb Carlson
Keith and Penny Carlson
Marlowe and June Carlson
Coral Dye
James Frazier
William T. Harding, III
Tom Woodruff

Tuesday Morning Men's Bible Study Group
St. Andrew Presbyterian Church, Iowa City

Recommendation

I met John Sellers in the late 1970s when he was working for Youth for Christ with at-risk juveniles incarcerated at the South Carolina Department of Youth Services. I was a chaplain in one of the facilities in Columbia during that time.

John showed great compassion and patience in juvenile ministry. He was innovative and was always trying new ways to reach out to the youth. He initiated soccer camp programs and annual basketball tournaments between the North and South Carolina Departments of Youth Services. He was able to secure community organizations to sponsor the events. John also started wonderful quarterly chapel services by using creative multi-media tools, and he frequently had dynamic speakers share gospel messages.

John was terrific in relating to the young people intellectually, emotionally, and spiritually. The ministry he implemented had a great impact in the lives of many troubled juveniles.

Chaplain Yu-Fong Chong
Retired Chaplain Supervisor
S.C. Dept. of Juvenile Services

CPSIA information can be obtained
at www.ICGtesting.com
Printed in the USA
FSHW021619080221
78384FS

9 781630 733384